HIGH PERFORMANCE MANAGEMENT STRATEGIES FOR ENTREPRENEURIAL COMPANIES

High Performance Management Strategies for Entrepreneurial Companies

RESEARCH FINDINGS FROM OVER 500 FIRMS

Rajeswararao Chaganti,
Radha Chaganti,
and
Stewart Malone

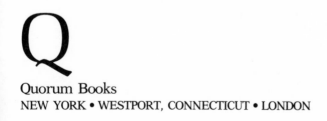

Quorum Books
NEW YORK • WESTPORT, CONNECTICUT • LONDON

Library of Congress Cataloging-in-Publication Data

Chaganti, Rajeswararao.
  High performance management strategies for entrepreneurial
companies : research findings from over 500 firms / Rajeswararao
Chaganti, Radha Chaganti, and Stewart Malone.
    p. cm.
  Includes index.
  ISBN 0-89930-561-X (alk. paper)
    1. Small Business—Management. 2. Strategic planning.
I. Chaganti, Radha. II. Malone, Stewart. III. Title.
HD62.7.C44 1991
658.4'012—dc20   91-8375

British Library Cataloguing in Publication Data is available.

Library of Congress Catalog Card Number: 91-8375
ISBN: 0-89930-561-X

First published in 1991

Quorum Books, One Madison Avenue, New York, NY 10010
An imprint of Greenwood Publishing Group, Inc.

Printed in the United States of America

The paper used in this book complies with the
Permanent Paper Standard issued by the National
Information Standards Organization (Z39.48–1984).

10 9 8 7 6 5 4 3 2 1

We dedicate this book to our family members, colleagues and small business owners, who made this research possible.

Contents

Figures and Tables

Figures and Tables

FIGURES

TABLES

Preface

There are several books that offer advice to small company owners-managers on how to run their businesses. Much of their advice, however, draws on the experience of individuals who assist and consult with only a limited number of small firms. While offering valuable advice, these books leave out data from the thousands of small firms existing in our economy. There is clearly a great need to add to the existing body of knowledge on small company management by systematically and scientifically studying those numerous firms and identifying the reasons for their successes and failures.

Some small companies are phenomenally successful; a few are modestly successful; others fail in their ventures. Small company owners—prospective and existing owners alike—can benefit immensely from others' successes and failures. Why do some companies fail? Why do some companies succeed? What are the most profitable strategies for small companies? Are there any natural "laws" of success and failure that are applicable to small companies?

This book is an upshot of four separate research studies completed at Temple University, Rider College, and the University of Virginia aimed at answering the above questions. As part of these studies, we examined the strategies of 532 small firms—340 in the United States and 192 in Canada.

Preliminary research work leading up to the findings and implications presented in Chapters 2, 4, and 9 appeared in scholarly papers published earlier by the authors in the *Journal of Small Business Management*. Chapter 3 of the book is based, in part, on the conceptual scheme that authors published earlier in *Entrepreneurship: Theory and Practice* (formerly *American Journal of Small Business*).

This book will be of interest primarily to small company owners-managers and consultants for these companies. Small business owners-managers can use it as a reference book, which contains lessons of experience from colleagues in business about the right and wrong strategies. Like small business owners-managers, small business consultants will also find this book a useful resource. This book will also be helpful to graduate students interested in researching the application of strategic management concepts to small companies, although discussion of the research methodology followed in arriving at the results is necessarily brief and simple.

Finally, we thank Eric Valentine, Executive Editor, and Diane Spalding, Production Editor, for their patience and support at various stages of publication of the book.

HIGH PERFORMANCE MANAGEMENT STRATEGIES FOR ENTREPRENEURIAL COMPANIES

1

Introduction

During the 1980s, small company management witnessed new-found prestige. The esteem and prestige are evident in the explosion in the number of textbooks devoted to small business management, the emergence of research conferences (e.g., the Babson College Conference on Entrepreneurship), the growth in regular reporting of news and research items of interest to small businesses in prestigious business media such as the *Wall Street Journal*, and the emergence of magazines (e.g., *Inc.*) devoted primarily to small company problems and issues.

Notwithstanding the growth of interest in small businesses, anywhere from 30 to 50 percent of all companies (with one hundred or fewer employees) fail within about five years of their founding. Although empirical evidence showing that systematic management techniques enhance the survival or profitability of small businesses is scarce, data of small business failures indicate that poor management, such as deficient bookkeeping, inadequate inventory control, and lack of market knowledge, may be a principal cause of most failures. A large number of small businesses, it appears, can survive if their owners-managers know how to manage—strategically!

The main impetus for this book is the lack of useful advice available to small businesses in the current literature. The little advice that is available is based on a small number of case studies, examples, anecdotes, or normative prescriptions. While these prescriptions are valuable in that they give an in-depth, clinical view of a small company's problems, the prescriptions cannot easily be cross-checked against the reality of what happens to a large cross-section of small firms. It is undoubtedly true that no two small companies are alike; but then it is also true that there are a great number of similarities in profitable organizations. Some small businesses become phenomenally successful, a few are modestly successful, and others fail in their ventures. Small company owners—prospective and existing owners alike—can benefit immensely from others' successes and failures. Currently, few books have gathered such large-scale evidence and documented and interpreted the action implications. This book takes on these tasks.

This book is about the linkages between a firm's business strategies or management systems and its profit. There are strong arguments for focusing on these key aspects of small companies. For one thing, there is extensive evidence from large companies that there are clear patterns in strategies and management techniques of successful firms. For example, successful large firms tend to choose to serve certain types of markets and use distinctive methods of management. What, then, are the patterns in relatively profitable small companies? Using a strategic management framework, this book provides answers to this question.

STRATEGIC MANAGEMENT FRAMEWORK

Over the last several years, the concept of strategic management has evolved in four distinct but related phases.

The first phase was *basic financial planning*, that is, regulating business operations by means of budgetary control and evaluating performance using a simple criterion of "meeting the budget."

The next phase was *forecast-based planning*. The essence of this approach is to predict the future and base actions on those predictions. Clearly, accuracy in predicting the future is the key to success. Both financial planning and forecast-based planning may be satisfactory in a highly stable environment and in contexts where risk of error is very small or even negligible.

In contrast, *externally oriented* planning emphasizes the responsiveness of the firm to external forces such as competition. In an externally oriented firm, management is continually driven by the environment external to the firm and the firm's performance will depend on how well the organization can respond to external threats and opportunities.[1]

In more recent years, the term *strategic management* has come to be associated with a whole range of activities involved in determining and developing competitive advantage and channeling the firm's resources for profit.

The strategic management approach assigns a proactive role to owners-managers. According to the framework of strategic management, successful owners-managers consider both firm characteristics (strengths and weaknesses) and external environmental characteristics, notably industry conditions (opportunities and threats), in formulating organizational goals, making decisions, and taking specific actions to realize these goals. The role of the owners-managers, therefore, is to continually align the firm's chosen products, markets, capital markets, resources, and suppliers with internal elements such as plant and equipment, technology, organizational structure, informational flows, talent, and reward systems.[2] Often this alignment is referred to as "strategic fit."

The assumption is that owners-managers who are able to convert their organization's distinctive competence into a competitive advantage will receive most support in the market and the firm's balance sheet will reflect that fact. Appropriateness of strategy depends in part on the market conditions in which a company operates, the competitive position of the firm (e.g., relative product quality, relative price, strengths and weaknesses of the firm), and the characteristics of the owner-manager.

A number of criteria have been offered in the literature to evaluation company business strategy. Roland Christensen and his colleagues at the Graduate School of Business Administration, Harvard University, suggest ten questions that may be asked to determine if one strategy is better than another. Although the questions were not suggested with small companies in mind, nonetheless a number of those questions are relevant:

1. Is the strategy identifiable and has it been made clear either in words or practice?

2. Is the strategy in some way unique?

3. Does the strategy exploit fully domestic and international environmental opportunity?

4. Is the strategy consistent with corporate competence and resources, both present and future?

5. Are the major provisions of the strategy and the program of major policies of which it is comprised internally consistent?

6. Is the chosen level of risk feasible in economic and personal terms?

7. Is the strategy appropriate to the personal values and aspirations of the key managers?

8. Is the strategy appropriate to the desired level of contribution to society?

9. Does the strategy constitute a clear stimulus to organizational commitment?

10. Are there early indications of the responsiveness of the markets and market segments to the strategy?[3]

In order to identify the strategies and management systems associated with small company success and failure, we asked over five hundred small company owners-managers questions about:

1. The industry's competitive conditions: nature and intensity of competition; industry growth rate (increasing, stagnant, or decreasing)

2. The organization's strengths and weaknesses: location, employee productivity, production capacity, product- and process-related patents, cash management, cost control, pricing practices, product quality, image of the firm, customer service, product innovativeness, distribution methods, customer credit policies, overall managerial competence

3. Product-market strategies: relative price, relative quality, percent of sales through different distribution channels, percent of sales made in different geographical markets, rate at which

new products are introduced and old ones are modified, size
and type of market segments served, breadth of product line

4. Personal objectives: relative importance of profit, growth
of investments, market share, excellence of the quality of
products sold, survival of business, image of the firm,
owner's personal satisfaction, employee morale

5. Management practices and systems in use: information
reporting, planning practices, hiring practices, use of external consultants, training of employees

6. Owner-manager's personal characteristics: age, educational
level, mode of entry into the present business, year the firm
was founded

7. Firm performance[4]

For factual evidence to be truly relevant to a large number of
small companies, the data must cover a diversity of firms because
small businesses are different from each other and the "laws of
success," therefore, are also different. For example, a small genetic
technology firm faces very different problems and opportunities than
a small lumber firm. Hence, we selected firms in different kinds
of businesses. Some were in manufacturing and some were in construction. Some of these businesses were run by men and others
were managed by women. Some firms were new, while others had
been in business for long periods. Some were highly profitable,
while others were surviving marginally. This book, then, identifies
the business strategies and management techniques that would be
appropriate for different types of small firms operating in different
types of industries and markets.

Also, to observe the unique problems faced by small companies
in cyclical industries, a separate study of ninety-six firms in the lumber
industry was completed. To examine the strategies for successful transition in family firms, yet another study of a select group of family
firms was completed.

AN OVERVIEW

The various strategy-performance linkages will be presented in the chapters that follow. In each chapter we will raise several questions of interest to small company owners-managers and consultants. Each chapter will include:

- A synthesis of the published research pertaining to the topic at hand
- Findings from the study completed by the authors
- The key implications for action

In chapter 2 we will categorize firms into one of two groups—profitable and not-so-profitable firms—and identify the key strengths and weaknesses, business operations, and product-market strategies that distinguish these two groups.

The focus of chapter 3 is on different types of competition and profitable small company strategies in each setting. We will distinguish four competitive settings: low-intensity price- and promotion-competitive environments; price-competitive environments; promotion-competitive environments; and high-intensity price- and promotion-competitive environments. The profit impact of four competitive strategies—cost leadership, technology orientation, product scope-quality orientation, and geographical focus—will be evaluated in each of the four competitive settings.

Chapter 4 distinguishes firms that are in high-growth, mature, and stagnant industries and identifies the profitable strategies in each industry.

Chapter 5 is devoted to a very special industry—the cyclical industry. We will identify the strategies that are profitable in the lumber industry (which is a very good example of a cyclical industry).

In chapter 6 we will look at the way the entrepreneur entered the current business scene. We will distinguish three modes of entry: start-up, buy-out, and inherited firms. Then we will identify the goals, strengths and weaknesses, competitive strategies, and management systems that have an impact on profit.

The focus of chapter 7 is on life stages of small companies. We will distinguish three categories of firms: juniors, middle-aged firms, and senior citizens. We will compare and contrast firms in the three stages in terms of business objectives, strengths and weaknesses, physical characteristics, and performance. We will also identify the management strategies and product-market strategies that contribute to profit.

In chapter 8 we will study family-owned businesses. Specifically, we will discuss "strategies" that are often used to perpetuate family firms. The role of strategic planning, the importance of family harmony, the role of the board of directors, and the role of the owner-manager will be discussed.

In chapter 9 we will look at women-owned enterprises. Particularly, we will examine goals, competitive strategies, and management systems that contribute to the profits of these enterprises.

Finally, chapter 10 will present a few strategy principles by way of summary and conclusion. Key strategy-performance linkages will be discussed.

NOTES

1. F. W. Gluck, S. P. Kaufman, and A. S. Walleck, "The Four Phases of Strategic Management," *Journal of Business Strategy* (Winter 1982): 9–21.

2. Charles E. Summer et al., "Doctoral Education in the Field of Business Policy and Strategy," *Journal of Management* 16/2 (1990): 361–98.

3. Roland Christensen et al., *Business Policy—Text and Cases* (Homewood, IL.: Irwin, 1987), pp. 129–32.

4. A brief description of this study and a copy of the questionnaire used can be found in the appendices.

2

The Strategic Profile of
Profitable Small Companies

According to David Birch, a noted expert on entrepreneurship, there are two myths about entrepreneurship that must be debunked. The first is that entrepreneurship is a get-rich-quick gamble. In reality, it takes a very long time to build successful companies: "you live fast, you die young." The second myth is that entrepreneurship is a gamble that most people lose. In reality, three-quarters of all start-ups survive.[1] In sum, it takes a very long time to build profitable small companies and the odds of failure are not as high as they might seem to be. What can owners-managers do to build profitable small companies?

AVOIDANCE OF PITFALLS

There is a plethora of factors associated with business failures. By implication, avoidance of these pitfalls results in success.

Pitfalls

Inadequate planning may result in failure. Poor planning includes making wrong strategic moves, such as selecting a poor location for business, undertaking unplanned expansion, and poor inventory management. Peter Drucker, a highly respected management guru, lists a few vital things that successful small company owners-managers do in the realm of planning. As an example, Drucker cites a successful barber-shop chain. The key factors to its success are location, traffic, number of people that can be served without having to wait, a team of trained barbers, and, most important of all, properly managed cash flow. According to Drucker, successful entrepreneurs do not go for glamor or bet on new technology but rely on the predictable things like demographics and population trends.[2]

Businesspersons who keep their plans in their heads or do it as they go are sure to fail. Instead, Roger A. Golde suggests the use of a simple "master planning form" to guide strategic planning. This form identifies the status quo and prescribes major moves that the chief executive should take for the next two years in such areas as product development, pricing, quality control, contracting with suppliers, and investments.[3] Other authors, like Herbert N. Broom and Justin C. Longenecker, offer simple and feasible management aids to small business entrepreneurs. For example, surveys by Chambers of Commerce and business journals should be used to estimate potential sales. Several simple procedures can facilitate economical and dependable purchasing.[4]

Insufficient capital, too much capital in fixed assets, inadequate records and financial knowledge, wrong attitudes about work practices or handling money, and poor credit practices are frequently associated with failure. Owners-managers can avoid failure by having the right numbers. Herbert N. Woodward recommends close monitoring of the sales, costs, and profitability of individual product lines so that products with relatively poor earnings can be dropped. Also, monitoring accounts receivable will significantly improve capital standing.[5] John Dearden details simplified types of accounting methods that should be used for profit planning. Cost figures, for example, should be typical and accurately represent costs that will be incurred by the firm.[6] In addition, management should require regular reports showing the contributions and net profits or losses for all products.

Unsuccessful owners prefer to do everything themselves and are unwilling to employ and work with a banker, accountant, and lawyer. They are hesitant to let go of things when needed. Success demands a wide range of skills—technical, administrative, and institututional—of owners-managers. Most owners-managers either are strong in one or the other and rarely strong in all three categories. Different skills are critical to success at different stages in the life of an enterprise. Ability to steward a new enterprise from infancy to maturity largely depends on the ability to see strengths and weaknesses and the willingness to hire outside personnel where and when help is needed.

Profitability and Profiles

Although avoidance of pitfalls is often recommended to avert business failures, such lists as the one presented above appear as "do-good" lists of small business practices. While such lists may contain a few sound recommendations, they are deficient in several respects. Most of the items in such lists focus on internal management practices and ignore external industry- and market-related issues and their bearing on a firm's choices and strategies. These lists do not point to the relative importance of various strategies and their contribution to the bottom line of the firm. As a result, entrepreneurs are left with no clear guidelines for action. A question that is frequently raised by entrepreneurs is which of several possibilities will enhance a firm's profitability. Concrete evidence of linkages between strategies and firm performance is rather thin. There are, however, a few good guidelines.

A number of studies based on Canadian data present some direct evidence to show that sound management practices and techniques have an impact on profit. Several studies have found, however, that few small and medium-sized companies use techniques like management information systems or formal planning. They do not employ trained personnel or participate in management training, yet they are profitable.[7] According to these findings, effective business strategies strongly influence profitability.[8] Our contention is that profitable small businesses have a distinct profile. These businesses pursue a combination of business strategies and management practices almost simultaneously and in an integrated fashion. From the standpoint of strategic management of small enterprises, identification of the profile of the profitable firm contrasted with the profile of the not-so-profitable business will be very useful.

FIRM STRATEGY AND PERFORMANCE

In strategic management literature, the term "strategy" is defined in a variety of ways. The definition offered by Roland Christensen and his colleagues at the Graduate School of Business Administration at Harvard University is very widely accepted. According to Christensen et al., strategy is the "pattern of decision in a company that (1) determines, shapes, and reveals its objectives, purposes, or goals; (2) produces the principal policies and plans for achieving these goals; and (3) defines the business the company intends to be in, the kind of economic and human organization it intends to be, and the nature of the economic and noneconomic contribution it intends to make to its shareholders, employees, customers, and communities."[9] The strategy may not be written in organizational manuals. It may not even be articulated for fear that it will commit the executive to a particular position, reduce the manager's flexibility to change the strategy at a subsequent time, or build organization-wide resistance to the strategy.

Whether or not one subscribes to the reasons for not articulating the organization's strategy, strategy can be deduced from an organization's actual behavior. Indeed, an organization's actions collectively speak to the actual strategy of the company. The term "pattern" suggests that strategy is not represented by a single goal, a single business decision, or a single action taken at a given point in time. Instead the term refers to a range of interrelated goals, decisions, and actions that have a bearing on the future of the enterprise. As such, we need to examine an array of behavior associated with profitability to identify the profile of profitable and not-so-profitable firms.

In both theory and practice, four levels of strategy may be distinguished. *Institutional-level strategy* deals with the relationship between the organization and its larger environment. An example would be the goals, decisions, and actions taken by a small company in lobbying the U.S. Congress to delete certain provisions of employee health insurance benefits from the present law. *Corporate strategy* focuses on decisions that define the businesses in which a firm chooses to compete, and decisions that channel resources to convert the organization's distinctive strengths into competitive advantages. *Business strategy* deals with decisions that determine how a company will compete in a given, chosen business and decisions that develop competitive advantage in that business. Finally, *functional strategy* focuses on productivity of resources in each functional area, namely, marketing, finance, operations, and human resources, and deals with goals, decisions, and actions that determine the utilization of the resources for profit, in the face of limits imposed on the corporation. For example, a decision to be a quality leader in the market is a functional strategy.[10]

All four levels of strategy do not occur in all organizations. In large, multidivisional corporations all four strategies are frequently formulated and implemented. In contrast, in small companies corporate and business strategies are made at the same level in the organization; consequently, the two levels of strategy cannot be distinguished. Therefore, for the purposes of this book, which deals exclusively with strategic management in small companies, it is appropriate to focus strictly on business strategies.

The specific strategy that a firm pursues depends, in part, on the characteristics of the industry in which the firm is doing business. According to the Profit Impact of Marketing Strategy (PIMS) researchers, who examined business strategies of several thousand large businesses, there are a few ''common denominators'' in all business strategies. The essence of a business strategy can be described by the following common denominators:

- *Product policy*—relative product quality, rate at which new products are introduced
- *Pricing policy*—relative product price
- *Marketing program*—relative advertising expenditure
- *Investment strategy*—investment in additional capacity
- *Workforce productivity*—employees to sales ratio
- *Vertical integration*—proportion of cost of goods sold supplied by company-owned plants
- *Research and development*—product patents used by the firm

Some of these dimensions may be key to profitability while other dimensions may be relatively unimportant or even irrelevant. Further, in our view, competitive advantage (strength) of the firm with respect to each of the common denominators, how well a firm performs business operations relating to the common denominators, and product market actions taken by the firm with respect to each dimension of the strategy, determine performance of the firm.

In this chapter we will examine three specific questions that pertain to strengths and weaknesses, business operations, and product-market strategy:

1. In what ways do the strengths of profitable small business organizations differ from those of less profitable firms?

2. How do business operations of profitable small businesses compare with the operations of the not-so-profitable leading competitors?

3. What are the key product and market strategies followed by profitable and not-so-profitable small businesses?

PROFILES OF PROFITABLE FIRMS

The 532 firms researched in our study were categorized into two groups based on their profitability figures. In group 1 were the firms that reported profitability of 13 percent or less (114 cases); in group 2 were the firms with more than 13 percent profitability (75 cases).

What variables predict the profitability of a firm? To answer this question, three separate discriminate analyses were performed, each using a different set of predictors. The three analyses corresponded to the research questions identified earlier.

In the first run, a two-group discriminant analysis was completed using the ratings given to the twelve items in Table 2.1 as predictors in order to determine the ways in which the strengths and weaknesses of profitable businesses might differ from those that were less profitable. The objective was to estimate a discriminant function that would best separate the two groups of firms. Relative values of the discriminant function coefficients are the measures of importance of the strengths and weaknesses. Standardized discriminant function coefficients along with the other pertinent data are presented in Table 2.1. The analysis was repeated for business operations and product-market strategy. The results are presented in Tables 2.2 and 2.3, respectively.

Table 2.1
Strengths/Weaknesses and Profitability

Strengths/Weaknesses	Standardized Discriminant Function Coefficient
Associated with Profitable Firms:	
Cash management	0.45
Innovativeness of the firm	0.37
Overall managerial competence	0.34
Location of the plant	0.32
Overall image of the firm	0.24
Marketing (including selling, promotion, and distribution)	0.17
Associated with Not-So-Profitable Firms:	
Productivity of employees	-0.61
Product quality	-0.13
Control of manufacturing costs	-0.06
Product pricing	-0.04
Not Associated with Either Profitable or Not-So-Profitable Firms:	
Customer service	0.00
Production capacity	0.00
Centroid of the groups:	
Group 1 (profitability less than 13 percent)	-0.24
Group 2 (profitability greater than 13 percent)	0.33
Number of cases correctly classified	63.8%

Note: Only statistically significant results are presented.

Major Strengths of Profitable Firms

A study of over five hundred small enterprises (results presented in Table 2.1) showed that among the twelve strengths and weaknesses

Table 2.2
Product-Market Strategies and Profitability

Product-Market Strategies	Standardized Discriminant Function Coefficient
Associated with Profitable Firms:	
Breadth of product line	-0.73
Patents and trade secrets pertaining to product	-0.01
Associated with Not-So-Profitable Firms:	
Percent of sales made in local (within 100 miles) markets	-0.64
Standardized product	0.34
Frequency with which old products are modified or new products are introduced	-0.26
Not Associated with Either Profitable or Not-So-Profitable Firms:	
Percent of sales made directly to customers	0.00
Centroid of the groups:	
Group 1 (profitability less than 13 percent)	0.21
Group 2 (profitability greater than 13 percent)	-0.33
Number of cases correctly classified	64.6%

Note: Only statistically significant results are presented.

examined, five strengths clearly distinguished the profitable and the not-so-profitable firms. The five in order of importance were: productivity of employees, the firm's ability to manage its cash, innovativeness

Table 2.3
Business Operations and Profitability

Business Operations	Standardized Discriminant Function Coefficient
Associated with Profitable Firms:	
Product quality	0.59
Product prices	0.49
Wages and salaries of employees	0.42
Associated with Not-So-Profitable Firms:	
Administrative and selling costs	-0.51
Manufacturing costs	-0.28
Centroid of the groups:	
Group 1 (profitability less than 13 percent)	-0.13
Group 2 (profitability greater than 13 percent)	0.19
Number of cases correctly classified	61.69%

Note: Only statistically significant results are presented.

of the firm, the overall managerial competence of the owner-manager, and the location of the firm's plant. Strengths in product quality ability to control manufacturing costs, product pricing, product quality, customer service, production capacity, and marketing either were relatively unimportant or did not make a significant difference in terms of profitability.

While the not-so-profitable firms seemed to emphasize productivity of employees as the firm's major strength, it is noteworthy that relatively profitable firms tended to have their strengths in cash management, innovativeness, overall managerial competence of the owner-manager, and location of the plant.

Product-Market Strategies of Profitable Firms

A separate analysis of product and market strategies (results presented in Table 2.2) showed that four business strategies discriminated profitable firms from their counterparts. The four strategies, in order of importance, were: breadth of the product line, percent of sales made in local markets (markets situated within one hundred miles of the main plant), nature of the product (whether the product is standardized for all customers or customized), and frequency with which old products were modified or new ones were introduced. Percent of sales made directly to customers or patents and trade secrets did not contribute significantly to the distinction between profitable and not-so-profitable firms.

According to our findings, breadth of the product line of the losing firms was rather narrow, perhaps too narrow for the good of the firms. Also, the less profitable firms tended to serve mostly regional and national markets—markets far from "home." The disadvantages and associated costs of serving distant markets seemed to contribute to losses. The losing firms offered mostly customized goods, and modified old products or introduced new ones only infrequently. The last observation points to the possibility that the firms may have reached a stage where their products lost "attractiveness" in the marketplace.

In contrast to losing businesses, profitable firms pursued very different strategies. The firms' product line tended to be very broad, the percentage of the firms' sales to local markets tended to be very high, and the frequency with which the firms modified their products or introduced new ones was relatively high.

Business Operations of Profitable Firms

The results from yet another analysis, this time of business operations (presented in Table 2.3), indicate that product quality, administrative and selling costs, product prices, and wages and salaries of employees are the most important aspects of small business operations.

The firms that did poorly tended to have relatively high administrative and selling costs and also relatively high manufacturing costs. In contrast, the most profitable firms tended to have higher-quality products, higher prices, and higher wages and salaries of employees than their rivals. Profitable firms seemed to pay much attention to the quality of their employees and seemed ready to pay higher wages than their leading competitors to attract quality employees.

IMPLICATIONS

Innovativeness, know-how, and creativity are important for success in small business. These qualities in and of themselves, however, are not sufficient for a firm's success. Small business owners also need to develop managerial competence as well, particularly in cash management. Technical competence per se is not enough; administrative skills are also required. Based on our findings, we offer the following recommendations.

Business location is an important consideration for a small business. Proximity to markets appears to enhance profitability for small businesses. To profitably serve regional and national markets far from the home base may require large, complex organizational structures and certain economies of scale that go beyond the capabilities of most small firms.

Performance of smaller businesses depends on local market conditions. Focusing on local markets and avoiding the logistic and organizational complexities associated with distant markets seems to be the most appropriate strategy for small firms. The obvious lesson for selecting a plant site and marketing outlets is to locate close to the market.

Entrepreneurs would profit most by building managerial competence in cash management and innovativeness rather than attempting to excel in all of the domains of management. Some of the strengths, such as cash management, can easily be acquired through training or by hiring trained personnel; however, innovativeness may be a lot harder to buy. Owners-managers who are creative and possess distinct "know-how," therefore, have the potential to profit from their strength.

Might managerial competence be the missing link in less profitable companies? If self-ratings of "overall managerial competence" reflect actual ability, this factor is certainly an important item. Managers of profitable firms appear to be more confident of their managerial abilities than the managers of losing concerns.

These findings suggest that both products offered and markets served determine the profit level of a small business. Stressing only product or market aspects limits profitability.

The most profitable firms appear to invest heavily in building quality rather than compete on cost and price. The rather weak contribution of cost to profitability is almost a blessing in disguise because most small companies cannot achieve the economies of scale that are essential to profit from cost leadership strategy.

It is extremely important to note that patents and trade secrets do not play a significant role in distinguishing between winners and losers. There is not much point in betting a company's future on a patent or trade secret. According to statistics on new product failures, even Fortune-500 corporations, which undoubtedly have deep pockets, superior management talent, and market power, find that every other new product idea fails. Given that dismal statistic, a winning strategy for small businesses is to use a proven formula. Kenneth J. Albert suggests several ways to do this: duplicate in location B the successful business operating in location A; purchase successful ongoing business (this beats founding a new venture); or differentiate a new business by slightly modifying a proven success formula.[11] These suggestions echo Drucker's observation on the case of the successful barber-shop chain.

In this chapter we examined the profiles of profitable firms and compared those profiles with the properties of not-so-profitable businesses. Profitability of a strategy, however, may depend on a variety of other considerations. For example, the degree and nature of competition may render certain strategies more appropriate than others. This issue will be examined in the next chapter.

NOTES

1. David Birch, "Live Fast—Die Young," *Inc.* (Aug. 1988): 23–24.

2. *U.S. News and World Report* (Mar. 26, 1984): 68–69.

3. Roger A. Golde, "Practical Planning for Small Business," *Harvard Business Review* (Sept.–Oct. 1966): 147–61.

4. Herbert N. Broom and Justin G. Longenecker, *Small Business Management* (Cincinnati, Ohio: South-Western, 1975).

5. Herbert N. Woodward, "Management Strategies for Small Companies," *Harvard Business Review* (Jan.–Feb. 1976): 113–21.

6. John Dearden, "Profit-Planning Accounting for Small Businesses," *Harvard Business Review* (Mar.–Apr. 1963): 66–76

7. R. M. Knight and J. C. Lemmons, *A Study of Small and Medium Sized Technology Based Companies*, report of the Technological Innovation Studies Program, Technology Branch, Department of Industry, Trade, and Commerce, Ottawa, Sept. 1978; Maurice R. Hecht, *A Study of Manufacturing Firms in Canada with Emphasis on the Education of Senior Officers, Types of Organizations, and Success*, research report of the Technological Innovation Studies Program, Technology Branch, Department of Industry, Trade, and Commerce, Ottawa, Mar. 1975.

8. Joseph Chica and Pierre-Andre Julien, *The Strategy of SMBs and Their Adaptation to Change*, research report of the Technological Innovation Studies Program, Technology Branch, Department of Industry, Trade, and Commerce, Ottawa, Apr. 1979.

9. Roland Christensen, et al., *Business Policy—Text and Cases* (Homewood, IL.: Irwin, 1982), p. 93.

10. Thomas Wheelen and J. David Hunger, *Strategic Management* (Reading, MA.: Addison-Wesley, 1990).

11. Kenneth J. Albert, *Nation's Business* (Mar. 1981): 83–86.

3

Profitable Strategies
and Competition

According to James Howard, a respected management consultant who
specializes in small company problems, one of the biggest differences
in running a small company in the 1950s and today is that businesses
today are more competitive. The margin for error is smaller. The
1950s were years of abundance and prosperity. Many undiscriminating
buyers and a great deal of pentup demand from World War II granted
virtual success to all businesses.

In contrast, the 1960s and 1970s were cruel. These were the years
of limits. In the late 1970s and the 1980s businesses were competing
with foreign competitors and the American businesses were playing
catchup. The 1990s are not going to be any easier. Customers are
more educated, more discriminating, and having tasted high-quality
goods from the Far East, more demanding. Combine these market
forces with the high cost of doing business, and we have a strategy
for tough times.

The quality movement set off by the foreign manufacturers is here
to stay. Foreign competition will get even more intense, the pressure
on costs will be relentless, demand conditions will be worse before
turning up again, consumers will be even more demanding of high
quality and service, and believe it or not, some mid-size and large
companies will compete with smaller businesses.[1]

Under such circumstances, small company owners-managers who
can understand the unique patterns of strategies that yield success

in different competitive settings can effectively lead their small ventures to high performance.

Small companies face competition in three principal domains:

- price of the product
- advertising and promotion of the product
- quality of the product

Businesses face competition in one or more domains simultaneously. What competitive strategies are profitable for small companies in different competitive settings? This question seems particularly controversial because there are differing views on the influence of firm size in dealing with competition.

Some researchers argue that small businesses do not have the resources to cope with competition. Therefore, strategies of those firms are driven predominantly by competitive forces.[2] Other researchers argue that smallness gives businesses the unique advantage of intimate knowledge of their customers. Consequently, the small businesses may be able to cope with rivals by employing differentiation and innovation strategies.[3]

EFFECT OF COMPETITION ON BUSINESSES

According to economists, price based competition often produces rapid price fluctuations in the short run as firms try to match their rivals' price cuts. When equilibrium is finally established in the market, the prices as well as the quantities sold tend to be low.[4] The implication for the individual firm would be that it sells limited quantities at low prices and profits, and hence is placed under intense pressure to save costs on all fronts (e.g., to minimize manufacturing, distribution, promotion, and R&D expenditures). Under promotion-based competition, firms attempt to reduce vulnerability to competitive assault by differentiating their product offerings from that of their competitors. Presumably, when rivalry is based on product differentiation, firms find the market to be stable. They spend large amounts to build long-term value-added features into their products through product research and development (R&D), customization of products to key buyers, additional customer services, and more attractive distribution methods. Economists provide conclusions on how different types of competition affect the market conduct of firms, but the conclusions place less emphasis on strategic choices.

Researchers in marketing, on the other hand, argue that the form and intensity of competition are determined by other environmental conditions such as the product life-stage or regulatory environment. Firms design response strategies in each of these domains to meet competition, and these competitive strategies have different effects on sales and profitability. For example, promotion-based strategies that attempt to reduce the cost of a product to customers tend to increase sales considerably in the short term, but may not increase the profitability of the product line. Again, the effects of a price-based competitive strategy are likely to be qualified by the fact that relative (relative to competitors') prices may connote quality differences in the customers' minds, especially in conjunction with the level of advertising. Some types of competitive strategies are more likely to evoke immediate and strong response from competitors than others. Further, the strategic options available to a firm vary depending on its market share relative to competitors' as well as the types of resources at the firm's disposal.[5] Hence a firm needs to take into account a number of interrelated factors in responding to different types of competition. While marketing scholars concentrate more on marketing strategy-performance linkages, strategic choices of firms under different types of competition have received little attention.

From the perspective of strategic management researchers, the intensity and type of competitive pressure are crucial contingency variables affecting strategy. According to theorists, rivalry could affect product-market strategies, an organization's structure, and administrative processes.[6] Even in the field of strategic management, relatively few empirical studies distinguish different domains of competition while examining the profit impact of various strategies.

PROFITABLE STRATEGIES IN COMPETITIVE ENVIRONMENTS

Four mutually exclusive competitive environments can be distinguished, based on the level of intensity (low or high) of competition in the price versus promotional domains:

1. Low-intensity price and promotion competition
2. High-intensity price competition and low-intensity promotion competition
3. Low-intensity price competition and high-intensity promotion competition
4. High-intensity price and promotion competition

What are the profitable strategies under each type of competitive environment?

Environment 1

This environment is characterized by a relative absence of rivalry in price and promotion. Firms tend not to experience intense pressure to build competitive advantage by way of cost leadership, product or process innovation, product differentiation, or product and market scope. Firms are not likely to experience a strong push to achieve market competitive superiority over their rivals, because a less competitive environment is relatively benign to all firms, and hence, firms may not strive to develop a single, sharp strategic thrust. Therefore, very likely strategy can make little contribution to firm performance.

Environment 2

In this environment, competitive intensity is high in price and low in promotion. It is a stressful competitive situation for small businesses because the environment pressures them to lower prices and may thus subject them to a profit-margin squeeze. In response to those pressures firms tend to concentrate on minimizing costs and avoiding high-cost strategies like product and process innovation and product differentiation, and on selling a limited number of standardized products. Relatively profitable businesses stress volume building, limited product scope, and other low-cost strategies, and matching competitors' low prices while avoiding long-term investments.

Environment 3

In this environment intensity of competition is high in promotion and low in price. Firms tend to experience pressure to achieve the least cost position. They can influence the market and build profitable stable segments through strategies of product differentiation or focus. Not surprisingly, cost leadership has no effect on profitability, whereas product differentiation achieved through emphasis on quality, customization, or innovation and the strategy of a broad scope contribute to high performance.

Environment 4

Here the intensity is high in both price and promotion competition. This environment is likely to place complex and intense competitive pressure on firms. In the face of those pressures, firms judiciously combine strategies that are known to work in price-intense and promotion-intense environments. Anticipating profit margins, firms tend to avoid strategies that call for long-term commitments, such as use of patents or product innovation.

Profitable Strategies

Based on a study of over five hundred small companies, we found that performance of firms operating in price-competitive businesses reported the lowest profit (mean = 4.80), whereas firms in low-intensity price- and promotion-competitive environments reported the highest profit (mean = 20.20). Firms in the other two competitive settings reported intermediate levels of performance. The performance of firms in the four groups, however, were not significantly different.

These findings strongly suggest that profitable small businesses can be found in practically all competitive environments and that firm performance in each competitive setting may depend on the strategies that each business pursues to meet the competition. What, then, are the profitable strategies in each competitive environment?

In environment 1, correlations between strategies and profitability show that profitable firms tended to offer a wide range of products ($r = 0.27$), emphasize customer service ($r = 0.26$), and build an image ($r = 0.24$).

Somewhat contrary to general expectations, profitable firms in environment 2 tended to minimize manufacturing costs ($r = -0.31$), pay relatively high wages and salaries to key employees ($r = 0.25$), and emphasize innovativeness ($r = 0.23$).

In environment 3, a wide range of strategies were associated with profitability, some negatively and others positively. Profitable firms tended to emphasize product quality ($r = 0.55$), focus on local markets ($r = 0.45$), pay relatively high wages and salaries to key employees ($r = 0.45$), emphasize the firm's image ($r = 0.40$), offer products at relatively low prices ($r = 0.38$), deemphasize innovativeness ($r = -0.37$), and emphasize customer service ($r = 0.33$).

In environment 4, the profitable firms tended to pay relatively high wages and salaries to key employees ($r = 0.18$), and emphasize the firm's image ($r = 0.27$).

IMPLICATIONS

Strategic management literature treats the intensity and type of competitive pressure as crucial contingency variables that affect strategy and performance. In examining the strategies that may be appropriate for each competitive setting, however, we should keep in mind that competitive strategies are comprised of a consistent set of actions in related areas (e.g., emphasizing product quality and the firm's image). A strategy is really a bundle of related actions, archetypes, or typologies.[8] Following on that conceptual lead, a number of separate actions identified in the previous section can be combined to represent three generic competitive strategies.

Cost leadership denotes a strategy where the firm attempts to compete by achieving overall cost leadership in the industry. This requires construction of efficient-scale facilities, pursuit of cost reductions from experience, tight cost and overhead control, and cost minimization in research and development, sales force, advertising, and so on.[9]

Differentiation strategy seeks to create the perception among customers that it offers something unique. Differentiation can involve design or brand image, product features, technology, customer service, dealer network, or other dimensions.[10]

Focus strategy involves specializing in supplying the needs of a particular product line, buyer group, or geographic market. As with differentiation strategy, focus strategy can take many forms.[11] Firms adopt one or more of the strategies depending on their specific strengths and weaknesses.

While there is substantial empirical evidence to support the existence of cost leadership and differentiation strategies, earlier studies show a lack of clear thrust corresponding to focus strategy.[12]

Results from an analysis of the competitive strategies of five hundred small businesses (see Table 3.1) suggest that four variants of the generic strategies—cost leadership, technology orientation, product scope-quality orientation, and geographical focus—are relevant to small companies.

A further analysis of the relationship between the four strategies and profitability (see Table 3.2) shows that profitable strategies varied in different competitive environments. Profitable firms tended to match strategy to the type of competition in the market. This was in agreement with widely reported findings in large businesses. There was one difference: in the context of small firms, effective strategies under the different competitive environments were far more similar than would be expected.

Cost leadership helped small firm profitability, but only in one of the four competitive settings, namely, where the intensity of price competition was high. Firms that had relatively low manufacturing costs were also relatively profitable. This finding was a bit surprising. Strategic management literature asserts that cost leadership as a strategy is not feasible for small companies as the smallness of the firm does not lend itself to the economies of scale that are vital to cost leadership. G. G. Dess and P. S. Davis have argued that cost leadership in general is highly conducive to profitability.[13] But according to our findings, cost leadership did have a contribution to make in a narrow set of circumstances, namely, price-competitive

High Performance Management Strategies

Table 3.1
Competitive Strategies of Small Businesses

Variable	Relative Cost	Technology Orientation	Product Scope-Innovativeness	Geographical Focus
Relative administrative and selling costs	0.63	0.04	0.01	-0.04
Relative product price	0.75	0.07	0.11	0.01
Relative wages and salaries	0.66	-0.28	0.31	0.14
Relative manufacturing cost	0.77	0.11	0.03	-0.08
Relative product quality	0.26	-0.06	0.68	0.09
Use of product-related patents	0.04	0.76	0.09	-0.02
Use of process-related patents	0.09	0.76	-0.07	0.09
Product innovativeness	-0.17	0.46	0.50	-0.20
Product scope	0.08	0.06	0.79	0.06
Geographical market scope	-0.13	-0.15	-0.00	0.75
Customization of products	0.77	0.19	0.09	0.08
Eigen value	2.40	1.59	1.30	1.10
Variance explained	21.80%	14.40%	11.80%	10.00%

Total variance explained = 58.10%

environments. Overall, attention to cost control was not a tool for success of small companies when price was not the primary basis for competition.

Table 3.2
Profitable Strategies in Different Competitive Environments

Competitive Environment	Mean Profit	Strategy	Association Between Strategy and Profit
Low-intensity price/promotion competitive environment	20.20	Technology (patents)	Negative
		Product scope/ innovativeness	Positive
		Geographical focus	Positive
Price-competitive environment	4.80	Cost leadership	Positive
		Product scope/ innovativeness	Positive
		Geographical focus	Positive
Promotion-competitive environment	12.41	Product scope/ innovativeness	Positive
High-intensity price/promotion competitive environment	15.57	Technology (patents)	Negative
		Product scope/ innovativeness	Positive
		Geographical focus	Positive

Note: Only statistically significant results are presented.

On the other hand, differentiation through product innovativeness contributed positively to profit in promotion-competitive environment. In contrast, differentiation through technology, notably patents, hindered profits in low-intensity and high-intensity promotion-competitive settings. In these settings, small firms offering commoditylike products may be better off utilizing readily accessible technologies than relying on patents and other highly specialized forms of resources and know-how.

A broad product scope, in conjunction with product innovativeness, significantly contributed to firm performance in the promotion-competitive environment. The finding reflects general demand for product differentiation in promotion-competitive settings. Small firms offering a relatively diversified product line were more profitable. This finding lends further support to earlier writings in strategic management, which showed a focus strategy does not contribute to profitability. Even for the small firm, according to our findings, a broad range of innovative products is helpful, particularly in promotion-competitive settings.

This result, especially when considered in conjunction with the negative relationship between technologically oriented innovativeness and profitability, suggests that where the more profitable small firms were able to create a product line variety, they seemed to have achieved this by engaging in very simple steps that add value, tailoring the terms of sale to customer requirements, and avoiding complex technology. It simply does not pay for small firms to engage in expensive product innovations or to use high-tech processes for product diversification.

In our pilot we found that the owners-managers of small manufacturing firms often did not make distinctions among different types of marketing strategies, such as advertising, promotion, and distribution. Accordingly, we cannot comment on the relative effectiveness of these promotion strategies. But overall, the administrative and selling expenditures do not seem to contribute much to profitability. Firms seem to achieve differentiation through means other than advertising and promotion.

In contrast to product scope strategy, geographically focused strategy was profitable in three of the four competitive conditions, promotion competition being the exception. In general, small firms are better off by serving local markets avoiding the administrative costs associated with serving markets far from home. This finding underscores the importance of a good location for business to begin.

It is noteworthy that in contrast to the multiplicity of the strategies employed by large firms for dealing with competition, there was a general lack of variety in the strategies that contributed to profitability of small firms. In effect, for small firms the types of competitive tools available for achieving these competitive strategies were far more limited than those available to a large firm. Therefore, the task of adapting to the competitive environment may be much more simple and, at the same time, very challenging. A few well-honed strategies may serve the small companies well in a wide variety of settings, but, then, it is very important that owners-managers are good with those strategies.

NOTES

1. James Howard, "Planning for a Decade of Problems," *D&B Reports* (Sept.-Oct. 1988): 19-21.
2. P. C. Khandwalla, "The Properties of Competing Organizations," in P. C. Nystrom and W. H. Starbuck, eds. *Handbook of Organizational Design* (New York: Oxford University Press, 1981), pp. 409-32; P. Kotler, *Marketing Management* (Englewood Cliffs, N.J.: Prentice-Hall, 1988); M. E. Porter, *Competitive Strategy* (New York: Free, 1980); J. A. Welsh, and J. F. White, "A Small Business is Not a Little Big Business," *Harvard Business Review* (July-Aug. 1981): 18-33.
3. A. Gross, "Meeting the Competition of Giants," *Harvard Business Review* (May-June 1967): 172-84.
4. E. H. Chamberlin, *The Theory of Monopolistic Competition* (Cambridge, Mass.: Harvard University Press, 1947); E. Mansfield, *Microeconomics* (New York: Norton, 1979); F. M. Scherer, *Industrial Market Structure and Economic Performance* (Chicago: Rand McNally, 1980).
5. B. C. Cotton and E. M. Babb, "Consumer Response to Promotional Deals," *Journal of Marketing* 42/3 (July 1978): 109-13; R. G. Brown, "Sales Response to Promotions and Advertising," *Journal of Advertising Research* 14/4 (1974): 33-39; P. W. Faris and D. J. Reibstein, "How Prices, Expenditures and Profits Are Linked," *Harvard Business Review* (Nov.-Dec. 1979): 173-84; K. G. Hardy, "Key Success Factors for Manufacturers' Sales Promotions in Packaged Goods," *Journal of Marketing* 50 (July 1986): 13-23; Kotler, *Marketing Management*; R. A. Strang, "Sales Promotion—Fast Growth, Faulty Management," *Harvard Business Review* (July-Aug. 1976): 115-24; G. J. Tellis, "Beyond the Many Facets of Price: An Integration of Pricing Strategies," *Journal of Marketing* 50 (Oct. 1986): 146-60.
6. Khandwalla, "Properties of Competing Organizations," pp. 409-32; P. N. Khandwalla, *The Design of Organizations* (New York: Harcourt Brace Jovanovich, 1977); P. N. Khandwalla, "Viable and Effective Organizational Design of Firms," *Academy of Management Journal* (1973): 481-95.

7. Porter, *Competitive Strategy*; Khandwalla, "Properties of Competing Organizations," pp. 409–32.

8. D. C. Hambrick, I. C. MacMillan, and D. L. Day, "Strategic Attributes and Performance in the BCG Matrix—A PIMS-Based Analysis of Industrial Product Businesses," *Academy of Management Journal* 25 (1982): 510–31; D. Miller and Peter H. Friesen, *Organizations—A Quantum View* (Englewood Cliffs, N.J.: Prentice-Hall, 1984); Porter, *Competitive Strategy*.

9. Porter, *Competitive Strategy*, p. 35.

10. Ibid., p. 37.

11. Ibid., p. 38.

12. G. G. Dess and P. S. Davis, "Porter's (1980) Generic Strategies as Determinants of Strategic Group Membership and Organizational Performance," *Academy of Management Journal* 27 (1984): 467–88.

13. Ibid.

4

Profitable Strategies in High-Growth, Mature, and Declining Industries

Well over half of all business establishments fit the definition of small. Given this fact, it is easy to see that these vast number of small firms operate in a variety of industries. Some operate in high-growth markets, while others do business in slow-growth or even declining markets. Statistics show that new small firms are usually restaurants, laundromats, beauty salons, or grocery stores. None of these are high-growth industries, but many of these entrepreneurships do well. Obviously many small business owners know how to prosper in mature markets. Therefore, types of product and market strategies that successful firms employ in different types of growth environments are important. On the face of it, it would seem that a business competing in a high-growth market will use different strategies than a business operating in a stagnant market. For example, the pricing and promotion strategies may have to be different; and cost competitiveness may be more important in some environments than in others. In this chapter we will identify the strategies adopted by the more profitable small firms in various markets.

CHARACTERISTICS OF HIGH-GROWTH, MATURE, AND DECLINING INDUSTRIES

In the typical growth industry many new firms are entering, so that the cast of characters in competition changes often; growing demand leads to high revenues; consumers are less likely to be price-sensitive; firms are more likely to compete in terms of product features such as quality; promotion is stressed rather than price; profits may be high overall. Also, firms can experiment with different types of product, pricing, promotion, and distribution strategies without provoking intense retaliation. In other words, these markets are relatively easy to compete in.[1]

Things will be quite different in a mature industry. Slowing growth means more competition, and firms can grow only at the expense of their competitors. Buyers have become familiar with the product since it has been around a long time, and hence are likely to look for better deals on price, quality, and service. Competition thus becomes more intensive on cost and service; profit margins fall. Distributors also may see their margins shrinking because customers are looking for bargains. In turn they will put pressure on the manufacturers, and this will further squeeze profit margins. On the whole new firms will not enter this market, but if some do, they are strong competitors who know how to do business in a tough competitive environment. A good example of this is the U.S. auto industry in the 1970s. Few new firms entered this slow-growth market except the Japanese, who were able to make big inroads because they had the necessary resources and market expertise to generate strong sales. In a mature industry weak competitors may exit the business. Hence only strong firms can survive and grow in these markets.

Declining industries, if anything, are even more difficult to compete in. The majority of firms experience reduced sales; products of the various firms become increasingly similar since it is too costly to invest in product innovation in the face of declining demand and excess capacity in the industry. Consumers are very familiar with the product and more price-sensitive. Distributors exert greater pressure for better margins, and may need higher inducements to stock the product. Prices and profits are likely to fall, and cost competitiveness may be key to survival. Such industrywide developments affect small as well as large firms, but the capacity of small firms to deal with mature or declining stages may be different from that of their larger rivals. In addition, small firms may sometimes experience growth, stagnation, or decline in their specific markets quite apart from conditions existing in the industry overall. For example, if the lumber business in one part of the country is doing well, the small lumber firm catering to regional markets may prosper, even if the overall industry is stagnating. The reverse may be true in other cases. In fact, for purposes of choosing the right product and market strategies, the small firm management may find developments in the local markets more pertinent than industrywide conditions.

Large Firm Strategies

In growth industries, a large firm has a broad range of choices in strategy. As we said before, large firms can experiment and determine the effectiveness of different strategies by trial and error. Many analysts maintain that this is the best environment in which to operate and earn profits. Firms benefit from the learning curve. The learning curve theory says that a company accumulates experience in doing business in a particular industry. This "learning" gives early entrants into the industry a critical competitive edge and helps them gain economies in production and marketing costs. High market share firms tend to be winners in this market because they enjoy economies of scale. Firms in rapidly growing industries often tend to invest heavily in manufacturing technology and plant and equipment because they believe that long term-oriented investments will produce even better profits and sales results in the future. They tend to spend on research and development to produce superior products. Firms may adopt a number of strategies at the same time. These various strategies become feasible because high revenues provide ample resources for investments.

Yet, when analysts look at the current profits of firms to identify the strategies that yield high profits, firms that have high long-term investments are not always the winners in terms of current profitability. The explanation lies in the fact that when firms spend for the long term, they are necessarily spending money and incurring higher costs in the short term. Hence near-term profits are depressed.[2]

In mature industries, the environment has intense competitive pressures. Firms have to choose strategies very cautiously. In these markets, different strategies are recommended for firms with high market shares compared to those with low market shares. The high market share firms would be better off relying on resource efficiencies:

maintaining high levels of capacity utilization for plant and capital facilities, maximizing labor productivity to increase cost efficiencies, and avoiding extensive long term-oriented investments in the business. They also tend to compete mainly in terms of price, and pursue diversification opportunities for future growth. If firms have a strong reputation for a unique product it is advantageous for them to compete by differentiating their products from competitors' offerings. One example of this is the strategies used by the two soft drink giants, Pepsico and Coca Cola. Firms like these can introduce product innovations even in a slow-growth or stagnant industry—especially if these investments in innovations do not have long payback periods. The low market share firm, on the other hand, is well advised to seek profitability through product differentiation or through niche strategies. It should avoid direct confrontation with its high market share rivals, especially price- and cost-based competition. Market segmentation is an attractive strategy when the low market share firm also has technologically superior products. Then competition cannot easily draw away its customers.[3]

A case in point for pursuing growth through product quality in a mature market is Rubbermaid Inc. of Ohio, which produces such mundane products as dish drainers and garbage cans. Yet in a slow-growth market this company managed to double sales and triple earnings over six years. Stanley Gault, the CEO, did this by launching about one hundred new products annually with a remarkably high success rate of 90 percent. The company attributes its unusual success with new products to constant contact with customers through focus groups and consumer surveys. Rubbermaid does not compete on price, but on quality and attention to detail. To make the customer orientation an everyday reality for personnel, the company carefully links its compensation system to results. Manager's bonuses are based on profits and workers' retirement benefits come out of profit sharing.[4]

Businesses are urged to avoid declining markets totally if they can. But other analysts are more optimistic and believe that firms can make profits in declining markets as well. It is even possible that companies may be able to revive a declining market. Even if growth does not resume, decline in demand can be slowed down. Therefore, unless there is a high risk of the industry dying a quick death, it may often be advisable for firms to compete through differentiation strategies (e.g., on promotion and customer service), thereby increasing the value-added elements in the products and building customer loyalty. In reality firms have to make choices depending on such factors as market share and whether they have cost advantages over their rivals. Occasionally, a firm in a declining industry may actually benefit by making long-term investment in the business. This can happen, for instance, when it holds a commanding position with the die-hard customers of the industry and other firms abandon these markets. We see examples of this in some high-cost, high-tech products like "outmoded" power-generating equipment. Customers who use earlier generation equipment continue to need parts, components, and service. If only a few firms specialize in servicing these customers, they will continue to prosper. Other options in declining industries would be to cut back commitment to this market. The cutback can be done at several levels, ranging from a quick and immediate exit, to milking the investment made in the business for short-term profit, to shrinking selectively in some markets and products. Firms have to make the choices depending on what they expect the future trends in industry to be and their own competitive strengths.[5]

Interestingly, many studies show that the same types of strategies tend to produce high profits under different types of growth environments. The *importance* of the different strategies, however, varies under each of the growth stages. To illustrate, under all growth stages profitable large firms tend to emphasize high capacity utilization, employee productivity, and high product quality. They also avoid huge investments in plant, product, and process research, or in building a large sales force. But, among all these strategies, two—focusing on high capacity utilization and labor productivity—are particularly crucial to profitability in declining industries.

Small Firm Strategies

Because much research has been done on large firms, it is not clear how far these prescriptions about the right strategies for growth, maturity, and decline apply to small businesses. On the surface it would seem that what works for large companies probably will not work for small firms. After all, they are so much smaller. They have far fewer resources in terms of capital, personnel, and physical facilities. Also, their market size is far smaller than that of larger firms so that very few of them carry the kind of clout that their larger rivals do with suppliers, customers, bankers, and the like. Even in the best of circumstances, small firms cannot match the long-term investments of their larger rivals in capital facilities or R&D, and entry into new markets is much more difficult for small firms. Yet smallness can have advantages. For instance, large firms grow only when growth happens on a geographically wide scale. Since they operate in limited markets, small firms can experience significant growth as long as their limited market is in a growth phase, even if the broader regional or national markets may not be growing. The CEOs of small firms may enjoy a uniquely intimate knowledge of their customers, which can keep these firms much more responsive to their customers' needs. Smallness also increases flexibility in the firm. For example, Harley Davison was unable to respond to the Japanese challenge as long as it was part of the large AMF Corporation. When it broke away from its corporate parent, it was able to quickly reverse the severe decline in sales. Therefore, we can say that prescriptions derived from large businesses cannot readily be applied to small firms. We should look for ideas from research done directly on small firms under different types of growth conditions.[6]

J. A. Pearce and R. B. Robinson interviewed CEOs of several entrepreneurial firms to understand how they managed strategy in different growth environments. They looked at how strategies were decided in each growth stage, and the types of operating concerns that preoccupied CEOs in each stage. First, regardless of the product's life cycle, CEOs of profitable ventures paid close attention to strategic planning. Further, they stressed speed of decision making and value profitability a key goals for the firm. But at the same time the operating issues occupying the CEOs' attention were different for firms in the different growth stages. Product/process design and achieving creativity were the chief concerns for the CEOs whose products were in the growth stage, whereas CEOs of firms with mature products attached much less importance to them. On the other hand, CEOs of firms doing business in maturing markets were much more anxious about dealing with uncertainty in the environment and avoiding the risks involved in product design.[7] CEOs knew that planning is important for success, as is quick and decisive action.

They kept close touch with the trends in their markets, and could identify issues that were critical to each type of market and zero in their decision making to those matters. They encouraged creativity and stressed new product design in a rapidly growing market because product innovations increase sales and profits. But CEOs in a declining market first and foremost were concerned with preventing, or at least slowing, the decline in revenues. They avoided risky ventures in product designs because they might jeopardize their current sales base.

J. G. Covin and D. P. Slevin found similar results in their research on what small start-up firms did when they entered different types of growth markets. One result clearly stood out: sales and profit performance of these new ventures largely depended on how far the venture's strategy and management practices "fit" (i.e., were consistent with) the market's growth stage. In emerging industries, the more profitable new ventures were risk takers in terms of product-market strategies. They not only made major changes in products quickly, but were often the first movers aggressively challenging their competitors. On the other hand, managements of firms entering more mature industries were quite conservative. Their product innovations were modest and they were careful not to challenge strong competitors in key markets and products.[8]

The Starrett Company of Athol, Massachusetts, a maker of precision hand tools, does not use the latest manufacturing technologies and remains a slow-growth company. But its 10.7 percent profit margin in 1985 was three times that of the rest of the industry. Starrett's success rests on its superior product quality, which has generated loyal customers. Starrett does not manage for the income statement but focuses on running a good business. Despite the increasing threat of Japanese competition, the company feels that its reputation and the aesthetic appeal of its products will ensure its survival.[9]

Small businesses in Montana in the early 1990s face the prospect of a slow-growing economy for quite some time to come. They should look for and exploit the pockets of growth, and emphasize operating efficiency.[10]

The case of Vermont Castings, a manufacturer of fine wood stoves in Randolph, Vermont, shows how attention to quality and niche marketing combined with prudent management of operations can keep a business successful even in a declining market. Compared to the late 1970s when the company could, in the words of its late president Murray Howell, "have set up a concession stand on the moon and sold them," demand had declined in the mid-1980s at 10 to 20 percent a year, and the Environmental Protection Agency was poised to introduce emission standards that could add as much as $300 to the price tag of a wood stove. Vermont Castings was profitable, however, and its balance sheet was healthy and sales had stabilized at $25 million a year. It was growing through acquisitions and diversification into products like trivets, fireplace tools, and wood boxes. The new CEO, Richard Clayton, says that as the need to burn wood passed, the company's customer base changed to those "interested in fire-viewing. They're buying a piece of furniture. They're attuned to colors, glass doors, brass trim." The new customers also made the company's new venture into enamel-surfaced stoves an enormous success. Having always been a top-of-the line manufacturer, the company is not worried about the new EPA standards. In fact, it is excited about its new design for low-emission wood stoves, which it expects will have great demand.[11]

Small firms, then, do not have to opt for the same moves that large companies make in the face of adverse market conditions. They can concentrate on building loyal customers through superior products and service.

PROFITABLE STRATEGIES IN DIFFERENT GROWTH ENVIRONMENTS

Our study of over five hundred small companies shows that firms in growth industries (i.e., industries growing at an annual rate of 10 percent or more) reported the highest profitability (return on investment = 18.83%). Firms in mature environments reported lower profits on average (return on investment = 12.35%). Firms in declining industries earned the lowest average ROA (return on investment = 10.81%). Therefore, it is safe to say that profitability is strongly influenced by industry growth conditions. Prospective entrepreneurs should study the market trends carefully, and select high-growth markets for entry. Even an ongoing firm would be wise to move out of mature, and especially, declining markets as soon as possible.

Growth Stage Strategies

Firms in growth industries, according to the results presented in Table 4.1, became profitable by offering a broader product line than their competitors, keeping costs low, and offering products and services that are closely tailored to customer needs and specifications. A broad product line gives firms a competitive edge because they can satisfy a greater variety of customer needs. Costly investments to gain sales and profits are not necessary. Strategies such as frequent new product introductions or offering complex products and services with proprietary know-how do not affect profitability significantly. Firms do not have to sell either the lowest-priced product or the best-quality product in the market to become more profitable

Table 4.1
Profitable Strategies in Different Growth Environments

Industry Growth Environment	Strategy	Beta
Growth	Relative breadth of product line	0.13
	Relative manu- facturing cost	-0.09
	Customized products	0.09
Maturity	Relative wage and salary costs	0.27
Decline	Relative breadth of product line	0.41

Note: Only statistically significant results are presented.

than the competition. Instead, they need to offer the "biggest bang for the buck" from the customer's viewpoint. And they can do this by offering customized products of reasonable quality at a reasonable price. It is more important for customers to get a product that meets their specific requirements than to get the best bargain on price or absolutely the best-quality product. For example, customers prefer a good, reliable, and convenient lumber company that offers a broad variety, to a competitor that has the lowest price or does not deliver quality.

Small firms can be as profitable as large corporation without using the same strategies as those usually prescribed for large firms. Large corporations in growth industries invest extensively—in plant and equipment, product and process research, and building a large salesforce and distribution network. These types of investments are quite beyond the financial capacity or expertise of small businesses. Yet small businesses can do well by using strategies that are quite different.

Maturity Stage Strategies

Only one strategy—high wage and labor costs compared to competition—contributes significantly to profitability (see Table 4.1). High costs obviously translate into the strategy of attracting and retaining a competent workforce. Firms in a mature market will not earn superior profits unless they are able to keep high-quality personnel. This is surprising, because wisdom has it that firms in mature industries do well be investing in product quality or through competitive pricing. Apparently, firms do not have to make these investments. Instead, they prosper by depending on competent personnel, which means paying them attractive compensation. For firms offering relatively simple products, personnel is the key to providing quality service to the customer. When sales stagnate, they rely on productive (not low-cost) staff. Interestingly, this result contrasts sharply with the strategies used by large corporations for competing in mature markets. Price competitiveness and resource efficiencies are effective for large corporations. Small businesses, on the other hand, apparently do not profit by trying to minimize costs per se. Rather, they should look for high-caliber employees.

Decline Stage Strategies

Here again only one strategy is critical to profitability—a product mix that is broader in variety than the competition's (see Table 4.1). As we saw before, this strategy is also important in the high-growth stage. The low overall ROAs show that competitive pressures are notably higher in this environment. Yet to remain profitable, small firms have to continue to maintain a broad product mix. In declining markets, just as in the growth environment, strategies that increase value-added elements to the customer help profitability.

IMPLICATIONS

These results give credence to the thesis that industry growth conditions have a strong influence on the profit prospects of firms, and that industry growth stage affects strategic choices. For large firms essentially the same types of strategies are profitable under each growth environment although some of these strategies (like capacity utilization and resource conservation) are far more important for profit in some stages (like decline) than in the others. In contrast, for small manufacturing and retailing firms, high-growth and declining environments require distinctly different strategies compared to the slow-growth (mature) market.

In general, in all three growth stages the strategies that produce better profits for small firms are different in many ways from those that help large firms. Large businesses act on a number of fronts, whereas small firms rely on a short menu of strategies. For example, large businesses emphasize employee productivity, high capacity utilization, and high quality, while small firms focus on one or two simple fronts. Small firms may satisfy diverse needs through product breadth, using simple and readily available product technologies. Small firms do not have to try and beat the competition in product innovation. They should make simple modifications and adjustments in products to match customers' special needs. This flexibility could actually give them an important competitive advantage because large corporations are likely to find it uneconomical and even impossible to bend to each customer.

Table 4.2
**Profitable Strategies for Small and Large Businesses in
Different Industry Growth Environments**

	ENVIRONMENT		
	Growth	Maturity	Decline
LARGE FIRMS	High quality	High quality	Low R&D and other investments
	Low R&D and other investments	Low R&D and other investments	High resource efficiency
	High resource efficiency	High resource efficiency	
	High market share	High market share	
	Low customization	Low customization	
Overall firm profitability	High	Medium	Low
SMALL FIRMS	Broad product line	High wage and salary costs	Broad product line
	Low manufacturing costs	Low manufacturing costs	
	High customization of products		
Overall firm profitability	High	Medium	Low

Firms should adopt different strategies in different growth stages. Small firms—just like their larger counterparts—have to monitor the market trends carefully and adapt and modify their actions appropriately. Responsiveness to environments is the hallmark of profitable small firms. A firm in a high-growth environment can pursue value-added strategies, but a firm operating in a mature market has to depend on the quality of its personnel for good results. Hence it will be unwise to sacrifice competence for the sake of economies in wage costs. (Profitable strategies for small firms are compared and contrasted with strategies of large firms in Table 4.2.)

In conclusion, small firms in all growth stages should be alert and sensitive to market changes. They should avoid costly investments and compete instead through strategies that exploit their intimate knowledge of customers. Firms should preferably seek business in high-growth markets, but need not despair if their market turn sour.

A broad product line and tailor-made customer service hold the key to success. When the market slows down, firms should attempt to achieve profitability through superior personnel. Obviously, firms cannot become attractive to quality personnel overnight. It is a long-term process that requires management not only to compensate the workforce well, but provide an environment in which they are encouraged to exercise their creativity and initiative, and in which they feel their contribution is valuable. Small firms should always pay attention to their personnel. Firms may wish to quit declining markets, but if they find that option closed, their best chance for success is by competing through a broader produce line that will not only keep old customers coming back, but even attract new ones as other firms exit the business.

NOTES

1. R. Buzzell, B. Gale, and R. Sultan, "Market Share—A Key to Profitability," *Harvard Business Review* 53 (1975): 97–106; M. E. Porter, *Competitive Strategy* (New York: Free, 1980); C. R. Anderson and C. P. Zeithaml, "Stage of the Product Life Cycle, Business Strategy, and Business Performance," *Academy of Management Journal* 27 (1984): 5–24.

2. Anderson and Zeithaml, "Stage of the Product Life Cycle, Business Strategy, and Business Performance"; D. Hambrick, I. MacMillan, and D. Day, "Strategic Attributes and Performance in the BCG Matrix—A PIMS-Based Analysis of Industrial Product Businesses," *Academy of Management Journal* 25 (1982): 510–31; Porter, *Competitive Strategy*; W. K. Hall, "Survival Strategies in a Hostile Environment," *Harvard Business Review* 58 (1980): 75–87.

3. Anderson and Zeithaml, "Stage of the Product Life Cycle, Business Strategy, and Business Performance"; Porter, *Competitive Strategy*; Hall, "Survival Strategies"; R. G. Hammermesh and S. B. Silk, "How to Compete in Stagnant Industries," *Harvard Business Review* 57 (1979): 161–68; B. Henderson, *Henderson on Corporate Strategy* (Cambridge, Mass.: Abt, 1979); K. R. Harrigan, "Strategies for Declining Industries," *Journal of Business Strategy* 1 (1980): 20–34; C. W. Hofer, "Toward a Contingency Theory of Business Strategy," *Academy of Management Journal* 18 (1975): 784–810; Porter, *Competitive Advantage*; B. Hedley, "Strategy and the 'Business Portfolio,' " *Long-Range Planning* 10 (1977): 9–15.

4. "Why the Bounce at Rubbermaid?" *Fortune* 115 (Apr. 13, 1987): 77–78.

5. Anderson and Zeithaml, "Stage of the Product Life Cycle, Business Strategy, and Business Performance"; Harrigan "Strategies for Declining Industries"; Hofer, "Toward a Contingency Theory of Business Strategy"; Porter, *Competitive Advantage*.

6. H. Gross, "Meeting the Competition of Giants," *Harvard Business Review* 45 (1967): 512–19.

7. R. B. Robinson, and J. A. Pearce, "Product Life Cycle Considerations and the Nature of Strategic Activities in Entrepreneurial Firms," *Journal of Business Venturing* 1/2 (Spring 1986): 207–24.

8. J. G. Covin and D. P. Slevin, "New Venture Strategic Posture, Structure, and Performance: An Industry Life Cycle Analysis," *Journal of Business Venturing* 5/2 (1990) 123–35.

9. B. Williams, "The Antique Shop in Athol," *Forbes* 136 (Nov. 4, 1985): 54, 58.

10. P. Larson, "How to Survive in Montana's Slow-Growth Economy," *Montana Business Quarterly* 25 (Summer 1987): 16–18.

11. "Resolute Vermont Castings Defies the Downdraft in Wood Stove Market, *New England Business* 10 (June 2, 1986): 43–44.

5

Profitable Strategies
in a Cyclical Environment

For every firm expanding exponentially, there are hundreds, if not thousands, that operate in more mature, prosaic environments such as retailing, wholesaling, and certain manufacturing operations. Most often, these firms' future demand is influenced by macroeconomic conditions, such as the gross national product or the interest rate. As overall economic trends move upward, so do sales. If the economy starts to slow, then business activity slows. Often the important question is not how to manage when demand is growing, but how to manage when demand is shrinking.

MANAGING IN A CYCLICAL ENVIRONMENT

Cyclical industries are often characterized by wide swings in demand and supply, causing windows of opportunity for growth in size and profitability. When the cycle is rising, business is plentiful and there exist numerous opportunities for expansion. A very conservative firm that fails to fully exploit the upside of the cycle will miss major opportunities, while the impetuous business may go bankrupt during the downturn.

Demand/supply changes in a cyclical industry are, by definition, recurrent in nature. Despite the efforts of macroeconomists, periods of growth and prosperity are followed by downturns and recessions. And the firm in the cyclical industry must always be aware of the seemingly inevitable downturn in cycle. Expanding too much or at the wrong time could cause a business to carry excess capacity and overhead into a period where sales may not be able to support it. Unfortunately, too many firms can adapt to one part of the cycle, but not the other. These businesses make exceptional profits during a period of expansion, only to suffer major losses as business declines during the downside of the cycle.

Ideally, a business in a cyclical industry should fully exploit opportunities during the up part of the cycle and then retrench and ride out the downside. This ideal, however, poses a very tough problem: the ability to identify both the amplitude and duration of the cycle (Figure 5.1). If a downturn is expected to be very slight (Figure 5.2), it is possible that little or no corrective action may be necessary. If the downturn is expected to result in a decline in demand of 50 percent (Figure 5.3), however, then major layoffs and capacity reductions may be required if the firm is to survive.

Aside from identifying the amplitude of the cycle impact, a firm also needs to identify the timing of the cycle. Even when experts agree that a change in the cycle is due, there is usually no consensus when it will occur. Yet this question is fundamental to any firm's planning process. If, for example, a severe downturn is expected in six months, a business may be able to reduce its inventory levels and eliminate its questionable accounts receivable in an orderly manner. Should the downturn be expected in two months, then more drastic actions are necessary. The need for accurate timing estimates becomes critical as the firm plans for the future or is involved in businesses where capacity is difficult to change rapidly.

There are three tasks that successful managers perform in a cyclical environment. First, they sense a coming change in the cycle. Second, they utilize a decision-making style that allows them to respond appropriately. Third, they select a strategy that maximized potential gain and minimizes losses.

Before owners-managers can do anything to prepare an organization for a different set of business conditions, they must somehow sense that a change is coming. This process of readying an organization for changing business conditions consists of two components: sensing

Figure 5.1
A Business Cycle

Sales

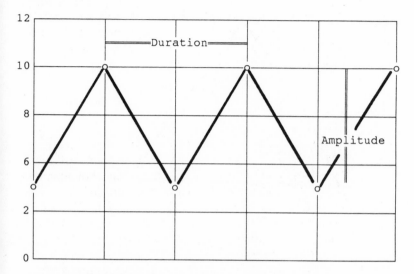

and decision making. Since in the present context we are referring to those activities of owners-managers that often require interaction with people outside their own organization, we will refer to the sensing task as boundary-spanning activity.[1]

Meeting with customers, negotiating with suppliers, or participating in trade association meetings are all examples of boundary-spanning activities. And if owners-managers spend a great deal of time in boundary spanning, then it is highly likely that they may sense the coming change sooner than non-boundary-spanning counterparts. Boundary-spanning activity acts as a type of early warning system for changes in the business cycle.

The early sensing of a coming change in the business environment is of little utility if the business is unable to respond in a timely manner, and it is here that the decision-making process becomes of critical importance. Two polar opposite styles of decision making have been identified. The first style, comprehensive decision making, generally involves a great deal of research and analysis. All possible options

Figure 5.2
A Steep Business Cycle

Sales

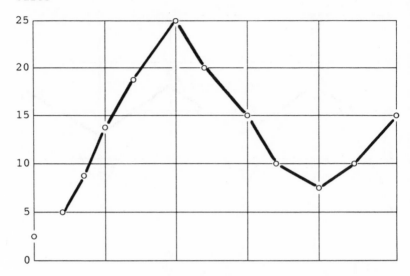

are explored and a great deal of time is invested in selecting the optimal alternative. Due to the thoroughness of this approach, it is widely regarded as a textbook model for decision making. Unfortunately, it is also time-consuming, and therefore, expensive.

The second style, incremental decision making, does not involve examining all possible alternatives, but looks at a limited number that would result in some small improvement over the current state of affairs. The primary advantage of the incremental method is that it can be accomplished relatively quickly and inexpensively.

For years theorists have debated the relative merits of these two approaches to decision making. Small businesses in particular were castigated for being too incremental in their decision making. The phrase "Ready! Shoot! Aim!" was an all too common criticism of the small company manager. Yet the comprehensive style employed in most of the largest businesses was also subject to increasing criticism as these organizations were perceived as bureaucratic and slow to respond to change. Some of the debate over the relative merits of

Figure 5.3
A Shallow Business Cycle

Sales

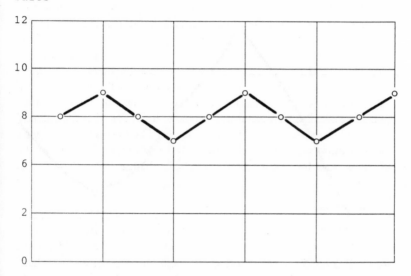

these two approaches to decision making was resolved when it was found that the decision-making style needed to be matched to the industry environment.[2] In a very stable environment where change is slow to occur, the comprehensive approach, with all its research and analysis, is more successful than the incremental style. In an unstable industry environment, where change occurs rapidly and unpredictably, the incremental approach is preferable. In the dynamic environment, the comprehensive approach leads to very good solutions to yesterday's problems.

The timeliness of the decision-making process is central to the task of operating in a cyclical environment. If the organization adopts a slow and deliberate style of decision making, then it will also require a significant amount of advance warning about changes in the business cycle. On the other hand, if decisions are made rapidly and incrementally, then less warning time is needed for the firm to take the necessary actions.

PROFITABLE STRATEGIES IN
A CYCLICAL ENVIRONMENT

Inasmuch as business cycles have existed for many years, it should not come as a surprise that both business theorists and practitioners have suggested alternatives for dealing with problems caused by cyclical changes.[3] Since each of the following strategies has its proponents and its share of successes, which alternative is the most likely to be successful? Surprisingly, in spite of the prevalence of firms in cyclical environments, this question has not received much empirical attention. We can hypothesize, however, that the relative success of these strategies depend on factors like the owner-manager's sophistication and risk preferences, the resources available to the business, and the nature of the cyclical change.

Status Quo

Describing a status quo approach to cyclical problems as a "strategy" may be overly complimentary, but this lassiez-faire philosophy aptly characterizes a large number of businesses. These firms make only minor changes in their operations during the course of a cycle, and even then, the changes are made in response to business conditions rather than in anticipation. In effect, owners-managers either ignore or endure conditions until they are forced to make a change.

The status quo approach requires little effort on the part of managers, and may, in fact, be successful if the business is well capitalized and cyclical changes are neither severe nor long-lasting. Status quo firms often show wide variations in earnings and liquidity, however, making money at one point in the cycle only to lose it as the cycle turns. While these companies may be criticized for not making the most of their opportunities, the greatest danger lies in the possibility that the cyclical impact may be more severe than these firms can endure. Quite often, it is the status quo firms that do not survive the deep or long recession.

Shifting Demand

Perhaps the key problem imposed by a cyclical environment is change in demand. If a firm gears itself for a sustainable level of production appropriate for the low point in the cycle, it will miss sales opportunities during the expansion part of the cycle. Likewise, an overly optimistic level of production incurs extra costs during a cyclical trough. While some strategies for cyclical industry focus on adjusting output to demand, a shifting strategy involves altering demand rather than output.[4] The basic idea is that efficiencies inherent in a steady state of production outweigh the costs of rebates or rationing during periods of surplus or shortage.

For example, the hotel industry shifts demand. The busiest time for these businesses is during the week when business travel is at its peak. The weekend corresponds to the trough in the cycle. Since it is obviously impossible to vary the number of rooms, the industry offers lower rates to lure weekend guests. Similarly, rationing can be used to limit demand. The recent success of the Miata convertible caught Mazda underinventoried. While dealers limited demand through above-list prices, the manufacturer rationed cars to individual dealers until production could catch up with demand.

Shifting demand is a useful strategy only when the shortage or surplus of output is temporary in nature or customers have limited alternatives for supply. While auto rebates may have had an appeal as a way of reducing oversupply in the short term, one need only look at American car manufacturers to see how enduring such a practice can become. Likewise, rationing or peak pricing may be an alternative during shortages, but customers have long memories, and once the shortage is over it is likely they will seek other sources of supply. As a long-term strategy for cyclical adaptation, shifting demand has only limited utility.

Prediction

The problems associated with a cyclical environment are greatly mitigated if it is possible to know when cyclical changes will occur and how drastic these changes will be. With this kind of perfect knowledge, it would be easy to manage credit, inventories, and staffing levels. Private firms and government experts regularly release a plethora of economic reports designed to forecast economic trends. Unfortunately for practicing managers, economists are much better at explaining cyclical changes after they occur than they are at predicting them. Yet formal economic reports are not the only bases for a prediction strategy. Since most smaller companies operate in a limited market in terms of geographic location or number of customers, successful companies tap into informal sources of information about the future. Asking customers about their future buying plans or probing suppliers about competitors' purchasing levels are important inputs into a prediction strategy and may be far more valid for the smaller firm operating on a local level than national economic statistics. Starting in the 1980s, there were wide disparities among economic activities in various areas of the United States. For example, Houston was enjoying an economic boom in 1981 while the Northeast was suffering a deep recession. Yet by 1986, the entire Texas economy was depressed and the Northeast was exploding economically.

Counter-Cyclical Opportunism

If a cyclical industry can cause problems for typical managers, it is also true that it creates opportunities. When business is bad and pessimism abounds, it can be difficult to remember that eventually the cycle will turn up again. Yet for those managers who keep this in mind, the trough of the cycle presents opportunities to acquire assets, people, and markets at a cost that is far less than what would be expended at the peak of the cycle.[5] More than a few fortunes have been created by these "bottom-fishers." During the 1973 oil shortage, the general aviation industry was slammed as private and corporate aircraft owners adjusted to the drastically higher fuel prices. Not only did aircraft sales screech to a halt, but the resale value of high fuel-consuming aircraft plummeted. A few brave aircraft dealers used this opportunity to acquire twin-engine aircraft at a fraction of their value. It was their belief that as the initial panic passed and users realized the usefulness of these planes, prices would rise dramatically. Ultimately, they were proved correct.

The practical problem with counter-cyclical opportunism lies in its dependence on prediction. Ideally, you want your opportunistic move to come at the bottom of the cycle (buying in at the cheapest price) and the move should come just prior to the cyclical upturn (so you do not have carrying costs across the entire trough of the cycle).

The case of a lumber company pursuing a counter-cyclical opportunistic strategy illustrates the risks of inaccurate prediction. In mid-1980, the ABC Lumber Company was suffering through the worst housing recession in thirty years. National housing starts had fallen from 2.1 million in 1979 to 1.4 million in 1981. As other lumber companies were laying off employees and even closing their doors, ABC's owner-manager saw a growth window of opportunity. Figuring that it would be politically unacceptable to the new Reagan administration to allow the recession to continue, ABC's president predicted that the government would soon stimulate the economy, especially the home-building sector. By acting quickly, he could hire the best salespeople and acquire new locations for a fraction of their cost, thus giving his firm a competitive advantage for the coming boom. Unfortunately for ABC Lumber, the housing slump did not end quickly, but continued its decline for eighteen more months. Saddled with the expenses of excess personnel and unneeded physical facilities, it took only eight months until ABC filed for bankruptcy.

The plight of ABC Lumber illustrates both the attractiveness and the dangers associated with counter-cyclical opportunism. Correctly executed, this strategy can offer a firm a quantum leap forward in its competitive advantage. Important skills and assets can be acquired at a time when there are few other bidders for them. Yet this strategy offers high risk as well as high reward. Also, the firm pursuing a counter-cyclical strategy needs sufficient financial reserves to carry the added capacity for a period of time if the accuracy of its predictions is in error. ABC's mistake was not being overly ambitious in its expansion plans, but expanding to such an extent that when the building upturn did not occur exactly when predicted, it could not afford to carry its new capacity.

Flexibility

Aside from the strategies described above, what other ways are there for firms to prosper across the business cycle? One alternative that is receiving increasing attention is the concept of strategic flexibility, or "the ability of an organization to adapt to substantial, uncertain, and fast-occurring (relative to required reaction time) environmental changes that have a meaningful impact on the organization's performance."[6] By employing a flexibility strategy, owners-managers do not need to be expert forecasters of economic trends. Instead, management adopts practices that allow the firm to adapt to conditions as they change across the business cycle.

If we view increased flexibility as the desired end, how do owners-managers build this quality in their firms? In fact, there are multiple avenues to increased flexibility. Before we examine specific practices, it would be helpful to look at some of the theoretical underpinnings of each of the flexibility types.

Strategic Flexibility Through Overinvestment. Internal flexibility is the overinvestment in underutilized resources.[7] To most managers who are concerned with the efficient use of their assets, the terms "overinvestment" and "underutilized plant" seem like something to be avoided rather than sought. A closer examination will show, however, how this type of investment can provide additional flexibility for the firm. Imagine a firm that, during normal business conditions, has been paying its employees overly generous wages. Later, as the economy starts to slide into a recession, the management needs to reduce payroll expenses and lays off a few workers and reduces the salaries in the remainder. If the firm had been paying the market rate compensation, the best employees may have responded to the layoffs and wage reductions by looking for work elsewhere. Since the company has established itself as a generous employer many of the employees may be willing to ride out the bad times in anticipation of prosperity returning. In essence, by overinvesting in certain assets, the firm creates shock absorbers that help cushion the jolts provided in different stages of the business cycle.

Strategic Flexibility Through Diversification. Rather than trying to cushion the shocks of the business cycle, flexibility through diversification attempts to avoid the major shocks. The concept of diversification may appear to be applicable only to large multi-divisional firms, but almost all business entities have some degree of latitude in the area of diversification. While there is a constraint on the amount of diversification a firm can undertake (depending on its size and financial resources), most businesses do have some latitude in choosing to diversify.

Strategic Flexibility Through Avoiding Commitments. A final method of achieving flexibility is by avoiding commitments.[8] While it seems commonsensical that avoiding commitments will increase flexibility, there are many seemingly sound business decisions that limit management's flexibility. For example, if a merchant becomes the exclusive representative of a certain manufacturer, the representation agreement may prohibit the merchant from carrying a competing product line. Likewise, the decision on how to compensate personnel also has commitment flexibility connotations. A compensation plan predicated on straight salary reduces flexibility by increasing a relatively fixed cost, but an incentive-based system inflates payroll costs during times of prosperity. Nowhere are the tradeoffs between flexibility and other business goals more clear than in the area of commitment flexibility. By reducing commitments at a certain point in time, one probably increases costs or decreases revenues at another point in the business cycle.

While thinking about flexibility in terms of internal commitment and diversification categories has a conceptual appeal, it is probably more useful for managers to think about flexibility in terms of the functional areas of their business (i.e., financial, marketing, production, human resource management, etc., see Table 5.1). Each of these areas offers numerous methods for increasing a business's flexibility level. The important point is to pick those areas where the long-term payoff from increased flexibility outweighs the cost of maintaining that flexibility. In our research with nearly one hundred small lumber companies, we categorized three areas of flexibility, other than diversification, that we termed financial flexibility, operational flexibility, and personnel flexibility (see Table 5.2).

Table 5.1
Methods of Increasing Flexibility

Financial

    Maintain excess borrowing power
    Maintain liquid assets in excess of immediate requirements
    Increase credit line with suppliers
    Lease assets rather than purchasing
    Make sure owner-manager compensation and dividend
      policy is sustainable
    Make personal assets available for business use

Marketing

    Reduce dependence on a few large customers
    Reduce dependence on a few major products
    Maintain multiple distribution channels
    Strive to develop "excess" customer loyalty

Operations

    Utilize subcontracting to a greater extent
    Increase utilization of plant assets
    Shift plant and equipment to more profitable areas

Purchasing

    Reduce dependence on a few large suppliers
    Avoid long-term purchase commitments

Human Resources

    Train personnel as generalists rather than specialists
    Use incentive-based compensation systems rather than
      straight salary
    Retain the ability to adjust total workforce size
    Retain specialists on a project basis rather than hiring
      full-time specialists

Managerial

    Encourage different perspectives within the organization
    Create "organization slack"

Table 5.2
Components of Flexibility

Ability to *raise additional debt* (a measure of the borrowing capacity of the firm)

Ability to *adjust working capital* through additional personal investment

Ability to *increase supplier credit lines*

Ability to *adjust throughput* without changing plant asset base (an indication of capacity utilization)

Ability to *adjust total compensation*

Ability to *subcontract operations*

Ability to *adjust workforce size*

Ability to *transfer fixed assets* to more profitable areas

Ability to *adjust sales commitments*

Ability to *adjust purchase commitments*

FLEXIBILITY IN A CYCLICAL ENVIRONMENT

There is little difference between successful and unsuccessful firms in the amount of boundary spanning activity. This is probably due to the fact that almost all owners-managers report high levels of boundary spanning. If we are to consider decision-making style alone, successful firms use a more comprehensive type of decision making than their less successful counterparts. Yet the importance of boundary spanning and decision-making style are difficult to appraise in isolation. Rather it is the entire sensing-deciding-strategy linkage that is of primary interest, and the relative effects of boundary spanning and decision-making style become more clear after we look at the effect of flexibility as a strategy.

While strategic flexibility has been proposed as a desirable quality, it is not our intent to compare the efficacy of the flexibility strategy vis-à-vis the other cyclical alternatives. Rather, our intent is to answer two principal questions: Does flexibility make a difference to performance? If so, what type of flexibility is most important?

Flexibility *does* make a difference. Strategic flexibility enables firms to earn a higher return on assets over the long run (both the upside and downside of the business cycle). While above-average profits are clearly desirable, most firms also want to maintain some consistency in their returns. The problem is making excellent returns in good years, only to experience big losses in bad years. These types of "yo-yo" earning make it difficult to plan for the future, and will certainly raise your banker's eyebrows should you need a loan at the onset of a recession. Firms with high levels of strategic flexibility not only exhibit superior returns on assets, but these returns also exhibit less variability.

As far as which avenue to flexibility is most important, the answer lies in the financial practices of the firm. Superior performers tend to have liquid assets well in excess of current needs—a practice that yields two benefits. First, these firms escape the high interest charges on debt that so often accompany a cyclical downturn. Second, surplus funds could be invested in financial paper to take advantage of these same high interest rates. One company, faced with deep recession, adopted the policies of laying off surplus workers, cutting inventory, and investing in certificates of deposit. The president stated that although it was not a very exciting way to get through two difficult years, it made a lot more sense to him than incurring expenses to gain sales that just were not there. And while it may be obvious that excess financial reserves are a good thing to have on the downside of the cycle, it applies as well during a period of expansion. Firms with low financial flexibility have difficulty meeting the inventory, receivables, and other investment requirements needed to participate in the upside of the cycle.

High-flexibility companies not only work on keeping cash in the business, but also in having it readily available for the business. These owners may, in fact, withdraw funds from their businesses through salaries, bonuses, and dividends, but these funds are kept in such a way that they can be readily reinvested if necessary. Likewise, other sources of funds are kept in reserve for the proverbial rainy day. Financially flexible firms are also able to increase credit lines with their suppliers, perhaps through a past history of prompt payments. Overall, high-performing firms show greater flexibility in the financial area than low performers.

Our results indicate that operational flexibility and personnel flexibility do not materially affect financial performance. The most likely cause is that there was little variation in the sample firms' responses in these two areas, and thus, successful firms did not significantly differ from unsuccessful firms. If we look, for example, at the ability to adjust workforce size, successful firms may purposefully decide to make this a priority ahead of a cyclical downturn, while unsuccessful firms are forced to adjust workforce size by the fact they cannot meet their payroll. A second line of reasoning suggests that the operational and personnel factors are really intermediate stages of flexibility, that is, that current flexibility in these areas can yield increases in financial flexibility in the future. Clearly, further research is necessary to examine the effects of these two factors.

Diversification is not a very effective way to build flexibility. Certain attributes are necessary for a diversification strategy to succeed. Firms with a high degree of product diversification tend to have more uniform (but not higher than average) earnings than undiversified companies. Given the administrative and marketing complexity required to serve many heterogeneous customer groups, the additional expense these functions require may offset any benefits for many smaller firms. For a geographic diversification approach to work, sales need to be dispersed over an area wide enough to be experiencing different impact of the cycle.

Flexibility as a corporate strategy is not universally desirable and generally comes at some cost. In those situations where change is either unlikely or very slow to occur, flexibility does not offer much in the way of rewards, and prediction, or even a continuation of the current course, may be a preferable alternative.

In industries where a "first-mover advantage" exists, the desire to remain flexible often means opportunities foregone—possibly foregone forever. There are only so many desirable corner locations for fast food stands. The latecomer will either get a less desirable location or pay an extremely high price for the property. In either case, the goal of flexibility can put the company at a serious competitive disadvantage. Realistically, however, the number of first-mover advantages in mature businesses are relatively small, and the increased returns associated with the flexibility strategy are likely to outweigh the few first mover advantages missed.

While failing to capture a first-mover advantage can quickly put a business at a disadvantage, the desire for financial flexibility can have an equally debilitating effect (although it will generally take longer to manifest itself). The typical scenario works like this. An established and successsful firm faces a major long-term investment, but hesitates. The reasons for this hesitation may be varied, but they all reflect an uncertainty or lack of confidence in the ability of the investment to pay off. As the firm's current business continues to do well and as the company does not invest in new opportunities, cash is either accumulated in the firm or paid out in excessive salaries or perks. In the short run, this situation is not perceived as dangerous. After all, profits are good, salaries and perks are enviable, and the company's balance sheet looks incredibly strong. The problem caused by excessive financial flexibility does not become apparent until much later when it is obvious that required investments in equipment, markets, and technology have been ignored. By that time it may be too late to rebuild the necessary competitive strengths.

Perhaps the most important implication of flexibility research is that all avenues of flexibility are not equally effective in dealing with the problems of a cyclical environment. Financial flexibility is clearly the single most important attribute in both contributing to superior return on assets and reducing variability in the firm's earnings. This has some significant ramifications in determining a firm's compensation, dividend, and investment policies. In prosperous times, it can be tempting to pay overly generous compensation to owners and high dividends to stockholders. Likewise, an aggressive policy of reinvestment may be pursued. Yet leaving the firm in a highly leveraged position threatens not only its existence in a downturn, but its level of profitability as well. The importance of a high level of financial flexibility is probably even more important when the downturn in the business cycle is caused by very high interest rates as in the period 1980–1982.

Does the importance of financial flexibility overshadow the other ways of achieving flexibility? While research findings seem to indicate this, such a perspective is likely to be shortsighted. It is more likely that some of the other forms of flexibility will eventually lead to financial flexibility in the longer run. Take, for example, a trucking company that maintains a fleet of equipment that is satisfactory for a moderate level of business activity. When the economy picks up, the manager could invest in more trucks to handle the additional demand or could arrange to subcontract the additional loads without purchasing a new asset (an increase in commitment flexibility). With the first alternative, the business may make more money during the good times, but may have substantial exposure to loss during the lean periods. Although the actual act of subcontracting may not have an immediate effect on profits, this practice may contribute to the overall financial flexibility of the firm in the long run.

For smaller company owners-managers seeking to improve their decision-making process, an increase in the overall comprehensiveness of the process will probably yield improvement, but an assessment of the firm's flexibility profile is required. With low financial flexibility, an incremental style is required to deal with changes in the cyclical environment. With higher degrees of financial flexibility, a more comprehensive decision-making process can be accommodated. But firms with low financial flexibility and comprehensive decision making are operating in perilous territory. They do not possess the requisite financial resources to absorb the stress imposed by the business cycle, and their decision-making process is too slow to adjust rapidly to new conditions. Financial flexibility is an asset that allows the luxury of greater reaction time.

Finally, flexibility should not be regarded as an all-or-nothing concept. Just as firms can build flexibility through a variety of practices, the level of strategic flexibility can also be managed to some extent. As a business matures and a downturn becomes more likely, an owner-manager may prudently decide to increase the firm's flexibility profile. Likewise, once an expansion is underway, flexibility levels may be decreased. While many areas such as long-term investments and compensation plans may be difficult to change in the short run, other practices, such as borrowing capacity and dividend policies, may yield significant changes in a business's strategic flexibility profile. The challenge of devising an optimal strategic flexibility profile is only limited by the owner-manager's skill, risk preferences, and imagination.

NOTES

1. Marc J. Dollinger, "Environmental Boundary Spanning and Informational Processing Effects on Organizational Performance," *Academy of Management Journal* 27/2 (1984): 351–68.

2. James W. Frederickson and Terence Mitchell, "Strategic Decision Processes: Comprehensiveness and Performance in an Industry with an Unstable Environment," *Academy of Management Journal* 27/2 (1984): 445–66.

3. N. C. Churchill and V. L. Lewis, "Lessons for Small Business from the Recession," *Journal of Small Business Management* (Apr. 1984): 5–17.

4. Jay Galbraith, *Organizational Design* (Reading, Mass.: Addison-Wesley, 1977).

5. Briance Mascarenhas and David A. Aaker, "Strategy over the Business Cycle," *Strategic Management Journal* 10/3 (1989): 199–210.

6. David A. Aaker and Briance Mascarenhas, "The Need for Strategic Flexibility," *Journal of Business Strategy* 5/2 (1984): 74–82.

7. H. I. Anshoff, *The Concept of Corporate Strategy* (Homewood, Ill.: Dow Jones-Irwin, 1971).

8. Aaker and Mascarenhas, "The Need for Strategic Flexibility."

6

Profiles of Start-Up, Buy-Out, and Family Firms

In this chapter we ask yet another important question: What are the differences in the profiles of firms that are founded by the owner-manager, bought out by the owner-manager from another entrepreneur, or inherited by the owner-manager? Owners-managers entering businesses in these different ways manage their firms in significantly different ways.

Why are these differences of interest to us? For one thing, the challenges, risks, and excitement in starting a new firm from the ground up could be quite different compared to buying an ongoing firm or taking over a family firm. For one thing, the firm exists initially only in the entrepreneur's mind in the case of a start-up. It is a unique creation. The product or service has not been created or sold. But in the case of both the buy-out and the family firm, a firm already exists and is competing in an existing market. The entrepreneur does not go through the same creative process as with a brand-new firm. In the case of a family firm, the new management often knows the firm well.

Of course, all start-ups are not the same. No two buy-outs or family firms are identical either. Some startup products and services may be unique while others may not be. Some entrepreneurs may have extensive business experience while others may be novices. Again, some markets are difficult while other are kind. In the same way, buy-outs can differ on the extent to which the purchase is financed by equity versus debt, or it is a business in trouble or a prosperous one.

This brings us to an important question: Is a firm's management likely to be affected by the owner's method of entry? Specifically, we are interested in finding out whether they pursue different goals, and use different business strategies and management practices.

PROPERTIES OF START-UP, BUY-OUT, AND FAMILY FIRMS

Start-Up Firms

Much has been written about topics relating to start-ups (SUs), such as how new ventures get started, the personality of the entrepreneur who is driven to create new ventures, the kinds of industry and economic conditions that help or hurt their survival, and the numerous problems that new firms face when they are young and in the later life stages. For example, one study showed that in the restaurant industry, the entrepreneurs who started a restaurant tended to be better educated compared to those who bought an existing one. Also, more start-ups happened when the regional economy was healthy and favorable: ample sources of trained technical manpower were available; private and government financing was relatively easy to obtain; infrastructure facilities for business like housing, transportation, and education were readily accessible; and the taxation policies encouraged new venture creation. Further, new firms started in high-growth industries were more likely to survive and grow.[1]

There are two overall business strategies a start-up can use: either introduce a totally new product or service or sell a superior version of an existing product or service. Apple Computers, the first company to introduce a user-friendly personal computer for the layperson, followed the first strategy of offering a totally new product. In contrast, Compaq Computers, which offered IBM-compatible personal computers at more attractive prices, adopted the second strategy. Starting with one of these two "overarching" strategies, the new venture then has to choose the best method to gain a competitive advantage over competing businesses. Firms can build a competitive edge in three different ways. The first is through *cost leadership*. In this strategy, a business competes by offering its products at the lowest price. The second is the *differentiation* strategy, in which the firm tries to distinguish its products from those of its rivals and makes them more attractive to the customers. It can differentiate its products in any number of ways (through advertising, extra services, warranties, better quality, added features, packaging, and so on). Third, a firm can decide to *focus* or specialize in catering to one specific group of customers or offer one particular group of products.[2]

Turning to management practices, we find that the types of issues that take up management's time and attention change over the growth stages of the firm. They also vary depending on the type of start-up.[3] For example, new professional service ventures give the highest priority to marketing and selling, then to financial management, and finally to general management problems in their first five years. But the concerns of high-tech start-ups in their early years are different. First and foremost is the positioning of products in markets, second is the people aspects, and third is the concern for building marketing and sales skills. After the early start-up is under their belt, the priority question for these high-tech ventures is the strengthening of marketing and sales, followed by the need to improve product positioning.[4]

Individuals who create their own ventures are supposed to be people with a unique idea, willing to work hard while undaunted by the prospect of failure. A story illustrating this point is that of Mary Evans, reported in *Vogue*.[5] She once worked for a very large investment bank in Manhattan. She left it in 1983 to start Gelato Modo, a chain of Italian-style ice-cream stores. Three years later, this low-tech business was very successful, with stores in New York City and New Jersey and sales in excess of $1 million. Evans got the idea for the business when she happened to taste Italian ice cream on a business trip to San Francisco. She went to Italy in search of the right recipe, and then chose the Manhattan location for her business based on market data from the Census Bureau. Being an experienced financial analyst, she put together a convincing business plan and raised $200,000. Evans was undeterred by failure. She felt that at her age she could start over, if it came to that. She was the typical start-up entrepreneur because the product idea was the primary starting impulse coupled with a personal conviction that it would be a success. Everything else evolved. Yet Evans was not the typical entrepreneur;

she had a very systematic approach that included a scientifically done market study, a credible business plan, and a strong capital base. Another example of a start-up is the service business started by Helen Berman. She created a business offering training programs to sales and marketing personnel. She decided to focus on the magazine publishing industry as the target group. She built the demand diligently. She spoke at industry seminars, wrote in leading trade magazines, and used audiotapes to market her expertise. In four years, her business was highly profitable.[6]

These stories tell us that venture founders are of many types. They create various kinds of enterprises, and achieve different degrees of success. But successful venture founders seem to share some common business approaches. They pick the right market niche and then direct all their efforts at marketing to that niche.

Buy-Out Firms

For the most part, the buy-out (BO) can be viewed as a variant of the start-up.[7] But some differences exist. The BO's profits can be better estimated, particularly if the purchased company had a prior record of stable revenues and profit. In fact, when this is the case the new owner may do well in spite of lack of experience. "If the acquiring entrepreneur applies sound management practices to the company, the results obtained, despite lack of capital or experience in the business, can be impressive."[8] The reasons for this success are that the employees have expertise, the physical facilities and equipment are in place, and the market and the clientele are established. Unless a crisis is impending, the business may be ready for the next growth phase. In most cases the prospective buyer-entrepreneur conducts a thorough scrutiny of the target firm's profit potential prior to the purchase, and examines the products and markets carefully before deciding upon future strategies. The net result is that choices are made in a systematic fashion. The BO's chances of success, as a result, may be relatively better than the start-ups.

As far as business strategies, the first choice is between going with a totally new product or improved versions of familiar products. The second involved choosing either the cost leadership, the differentiation, or the focus approach to competitive advantage. BOs may be constrained somewhat because the purchased firm would already have a strategy in place. If the new management wishes to shift gears, it has to first dismantle existing product and market commitments. This can be a long and difficult task, demanding both financial and management resources. It may take time to convince the customers that the new offerings and services are superior, especially if the earlier products were rated poorly. Management procedures and systems BO's use, according to W. B. Gartner, seem to be of little concern to buyers-entrepreneurs.[9]

The case of Robin De Graff, who bought Extol of Ohio, an insulation-fabricating company in Sandusky, exemplifies what we have been saying. She was a long-time secretary at the company when it was put up for sale. She felt that, since she was an insider, she could better manage the business with the help of nine experienced and able executives in the firm. She was turned down by five banks for financing the buy-out, but she continually upgraded her plan to show that she was knowledgeable and could make key decisions about products, customer accounts, and managing people. It was a tremendous advantage that she could leave production and day-to-day business aspects in the hands of trusted employees, while she learned about the business by selling in the field. She advised would-be entrepreneurs to actively seek help from experts in the first few years of business.[10]

Randall J. Wall, a corporate executive, found his experience valuable when he and a group of investors bought International Medical Systems Ltd., a medical products concern, in August 1988. One of its products is a needle with a plastic sheath to prevent the accidental punctures that pose a major hazard for health care workers in the 1990s. Earlier, the company did not succeed in spite of its timely product, because this family-owned company had not devised a systematic plan to manufacture and market the product. The new management had to invest over $50 million to improve manufacturing operations, including installing a computerized environment control system, instituting training programs for employees, and obtaining new security systems. They had to rebuild relations with several major customers, such as hospitals and large health products purchasing companies, which had been soured by repeated problems in the timely filling of orders. The new management approaches strategy and marketing in a truly large company style, promoting the product heavily in well-designed brochures and using direct mail to over six thousand hospital and clinics. The early results are promising.[11] While the results can be remarkable if the mix of strategies and systems is chosen wisely, sometimes the results can be disastrous, especially if the new owner-manager is inexperienced and unprepared for the long and hard job of entrepreneurship.

Family Firms

Here, as with the buy-out's owner, the entrepreneur enters a pre-existing business, and then has the task of either maintaining and improving profitability and sales growth, or turning around a poor sales and profit situation. The entrepreneur also must make a choice between letting things continue to run the way they were in the past, or making radical changes.

In terms of the types of business strategies they might pursue, the basic choices are the same as for SUs or BOs, that is, whether to offer new versus existing products, and whether to use the differentiation, focus, or cost leadership approach. Ideally, all firms, regardless of the owner's mode of entry, should choose the strategies after considering the competition, the state of the economy, and the firm's strengths and weaknesses.

While this would be the logical way of selecting the firm's business strategies, reality can be different. Entrepreneurs who inherit family firms (FFs) may continue past strategies out of loyalty and look for stability in clientele, products, and markets without ever questioning whether these would work well in the future. Heirs who blindly cling to the past can bring disastrous results. When film-maker Walt Disney died in 1966, his brother and son-in-law ran the business for a few years. During these years, the only yardstick was "what Walt would have done." The company continued to produce family-oriented movies even though the audience had turned away from them. The company revived only when outside management replaced the family members following an acquisition battle.[12]

Several distinctive strengths characterize many successful family firms like Neiman–Marcus and Marriott Corporation. Top managements of family-run companies are more likely to take a longer strategic perspective. "They are more humane to their employees, they have a strong work ethic and they worry a helluva lot more about quality because the boss's name is on the product."[13] Family businesses are better at riding out recessions and, less bothered by outside stockholders, they are more able and willing to sacrifice short-term profits for long-range moves that enable the company to be more responsive to a changing market. President John Norris of Lennox Industries of Dallas, a family-owned and -managed firm, says, "We can move faster when the opportunities arise, because we don't have much red tape. There are no political duchies that fight each other."[14] Family firms successfully build an image of product quality and customer service because family pride is often identified with the market image of the firm. When this is true, quality emphasis may become the hallmark of business strategy.

One major management issue in the family firm is that the inheritor-entrepreneur needs to be concerned with the interface between the family and the business.[15] When there is a transfer of ownership and control within the family, the new chief executive is almost always a member of the family. As Curtis Carlson, the head of the Radisson hotel empire puts it, the question is not why a son or son-in-law should be promoted, but rather, "what you look for is why he shouldn't be."[16] All is well if the heir is accepted by the nonfamily staff, but this does not always happen for a variety of reasons (e.g., if the nonfamily members aspired to the top position, or when they do not consider the heir worthy of the top position). In such cases, the firm may lose valuable managers who are embittered by the nepotism and blocked advancement. In fact, the most successful family firms take precautions against these problems by following the principle of meritocratic nepotism, whereby the prospective heir is asked to prove himself or herself in other organizations before moving into the family business.

With respect to their internal management practices, studies done on family firms show that on the negative side, many of these owners attach little weight to practices like future planning, systems and procedures, or professional managers if these were not part of past practice. Successful owners tend to enjoy the advantages of open communication among all employees. There is an absence of hierarchical structure so that the employees feel management is truly interested in their opinions. Also a "family" feeling prevails among personnel, leading to strong loyalty and commitment to the firm's well-being.

One of many examples of how to succeed by keeping it all in the family is the story of Brown–Forman, the highly successful distiller firm in Louisville, Kentucky. The Browns are a genteel family, conscious of their standing in the community and jealous of the firm's reputation. Meritocratic nepotism is the management rule in this family. In the several decades that it has been in business, this company successfully introduced and nurtured a number of products, including Jack Daniel's, Canadian Mist, and Southern Comfort. Their rate of return over the past decade has been 21 percent per annum. How do they do it? The chief executives, who are all members of the Brown family, carefully review every key product and marketing decision. For example, the top management deliberated for several days before giving a go-ahead to redesign the Southern Comfort bottle to broaden its appeal to women. Top management holds each brand manager strictly accountable for profit and sales results, and they put their budgets through extremely thorough reviews. They build a brand through heavy and patient advertising and promotion, follow the slow-but-sure approach to decisions, and adhere to consistency and quality in products.[17]

Now let us look at the story of a much smaller family firm, an industrial products company in the Midwest. This company was started originally with the explicit idea of being an asset to the city and the community. It would increase in growth only along the lines that experience had shown to be conservative. The company was to be owned and controlled in community and run like the community, with the traits of "punctuality, honesty, trustworthiness, donating of self, teaching by example, and having a firm idea of right and wrong."[18] The workers felt they were part of the family, and morale and performance were high.

Both these stories demonstrate that family firms can offer a uniquely superior product as well as achieve high productivity, and they can do this through a hands-on, caring style of management. Large family firms use sophisticated and advanced management methods, while smaller ones rely on personalized approaches.

DIFFERENCES AMONG SUs, BOs, AND FFs

Differences can be found among SUs, BOs, and FFs, such as key personal and business goals or issues that preoccupy owners-managers. Yet, we have no evidence whether these differences would cause these entrepreneurs to manage their firms' strategies and operations differently. Logically we can argue both for and against why there should be differences in their strategic management patterns. SUs, BOs, and FFs may have similar goals, strategies, and systems because, after all, every owner-manager is interested in being viable and will choose business strategies appropriate to the types of markets they face. Management practices will depend on the size and complexity of operations. On the other hand, we can argue that their objectives, strategies, and systems will be unique because owners-managers are different. We need to look at the facts from a number of start-ups, buy-outs, and family firms to come to some firm conclusions on to what extent (if any) each group is both similar and different from the other in goals, strategies, and systems.[19]

We know that no two start-ups, buy-outs, or family firms are exactly alike. It may very well be that all three types of firms operate in much the same way. But to the extent that we expect differences, what would they be like?

It is a common belief that entrepreneurs who start their own firms are motivated by a strong desire for personal satisfaction and self-expression. Therefore, in start-ups, personal satisfaction is a far more important business objective than, say, profit. In terms of business strategies, as brand new firms, these organizations may find the strategy of offering new and innovative products to be the best approach. Cost leadership will be an unlikely choice, because few young firms have either the volume of demand or the resources necessary for building superior cost economies. That is, differentiation by quality and novelty is the preferred approach. In line with this strategy, these firms seek strengths in innovativeness, quality, and customer service. Also they prefer to compete in a market niche. That is, they combine differentiation and focus strategies. Their systems and procedures are informal, both because they are young and because the founder may prefer to be self-reliant and retain full control of the firm. For the same reasons, they seldom employ professionally trained management staff and typically avoid long-range planning.

Family firms offer a strong contrast. For the most part these firms have inherited products with a stable customer base. The heirs adopt a conservative strategy, trying to preserve customers and markets mainly by price and cost competitiveness. Being quite old, they probably find it necessary to use regular and written reporting, but otherwise they are not receptive to the idea of instituting systematic procedures, unless these procedures were being used by their predecessors.

The buy-out entrepreneur may lie somewhere between the family firm and the founder's firm. The entrepreneur probably preferred this route for reasons of profit, and hence may emphasize cost efficiencies and systematic procedures. There may not be a particular preferred strategy, since entrepreneurs are more attuned to choosing the right strategy for the market. The business is likely to be run in a systematic fashion and there are usually well developed management practices in reporting, planning, and staffing.

The life-stage concept relating to how a business's strategies, systems, and structures evolve over the course of its life also suggests similar patterns.[20] Younger firms tend to be less formalized and more innovative than the more established firms. Typically the start-ups operate in earlier stages of evolution compared to either the buy-outs or the family firms (see Table 6.1).

About 60 percent of over five hundred firms we surveyed were start-up (SU) firms, 20 percent were buy-out (BO) firms, and 20 percent were family firms (FFs). The SUs were the youngest (11.88 years in age), FFs were the oldest (30.09 years in age), and BOs were in the middle (13.40 years of age). The differences in age were statistically significant. The average annual sales were smallest for SUs ($610,875); the BOs were the largest ($760,317 sales); and FFs were placed in the middle ($735,208 in sales).

We will first look at the general profiles for each group of firms in terms of objectives, strategies, strengths, and management systems, and then go on to discuss the differences and similarities among these three groups.

Start-Ups

Objectives. Achieving excellence in product quality is the preeminent business objective for SUs, closely followed by desire for high profitability and survival of the firm. Image of the firm in the market ranks fourth with the goal of achieving personal satisfaction fifth.

Key strengths of the firm. SUs consider themselves strongest in delivering product quality. Next in order of importance are customer service, maintaining a favorable image in the market, and product pricing. They also see strengths in productivity and innovativeness, but these are not at the top of the list.

Business strategies. Quality-based differentiation is the primary strategy of SUs and this is accompanied by a strong low-cost orientation. Compared to buy-outs and family firms, the founders' firms do not offer complex types of products, and the majority of their customers are drawn from within a one hundred-mile radius. That is, they cater to local markets offering higher-quality products that are customized, and they make it a point to offer a broad variety of products. They do not rate innovation as a key strength, yet they innovate often. They perceive themselves to be strong in areas that are key to their product and market strategies of offering quality, customization, and broad product scope. Start-ups stress a varied product mix made up of relatively simple and cost-competitive products of comparable quality. Their product offering probably matches the needs of the market in low- and medium-tech businesses, and the geographic scope of the markets served by the firms. It appears that many start-ups cater to local customers in nearby markets and these customers patronize businesses that offer a broad variety of relatively simple products customized to meet their diverse needs. Overall, there is a good match between their objectives, organizational strengths, and strategies.

Management practices. The use of systematic management practices is medium in each of the three areas of reporting, planning horizon, and hiring of trained staff. Their use of these practices is higher than the level of use in the family firms, but lower than that in BOs. Within the SUs per se, accounting and finance is the most systematized area, followed by production. For example, reporting is most formalized in the accounting area and least rigorous in sales

Table 6.1
Mode of Entry and Firm Characteristics

	Mode of Entry		
	Start-Up	Buy-Out	Family Firm
Goals			
1. Profit	4.28	4.06	4.26 *
2. Growth of investment	3.64	3.20	3.72 *
3. Market share	2.96	2.85	3.12
4. Excellence of product	4.42	4.13	4.52 *
5. Survival of firm	4.11	3.61	4.11 *
6. Image of firm	4.01	3.36	3.84 *
7. Personal satisfaction	3.91	3.12	3.75 *
Strength of Firm			
1. Location	3.34	3.49	3.20
2. Cash management	3.20	3.10	3.35
3. Product pricing	3.65	3.33	3.72 *
4. Product quality	4.39	4.21	4.32
5. Image of firm	4.14	3.84	4.09 *
6. Customer service	4.30	4.06	4.22 *
7. Innovativeness	3.48	2.82	3.16 *
8. Marketing	2.99	2.82	2.81
9. Control of manufacturing	2.96	2.63	2.98 *
10. Production capacity	2.98	2.81	3.07
11. Productivity	3.63	3.24	3.48 *
12. Overall management competence	3.45	3.29	3.50
Strategies			
1. Low cost orientation	-0.06	-0.01	0.31
2. Technology orientation	-0.04	0.11	0.01
3. Product-scope quality	-0.10	-0.12	-0.26
4. Geographic focus	0.03	0.15	-0.14

Table 6.1 (Continued)

	Mode of Entry:		
	Start-Up	Buy-Out	Family Firm

Management Practices

Reporting

1. Accounts payable and receivable	2.43	2.52	2.23	*
2. Manufacturing costs	2.10	2.26	2.09	
3. Profit	2.25	2.29	2.23	
4. Cash flow	2.27	2.41	2.23	
5. Sales	2.16	2.31	2.26	

Planning Horizon

1. Capital projects	2.80	3.01	3.02	
2. Cash	1.75	1.95	1.16	
3. Product sales	1.92	2.14	1.90	
4. New products	2.14	2.26	2.05	
5. New market entry	2.34	2.76	2.31	*
6. Staffing/Hiring	1.63	1.83	1.73	

Hiring of Professional Staff

1. Accounting/ Bookkeeping	0.55	0.72	0.63	*
2. Production costs	0.40	0.66	0.40	*
3. Marketing/Sales	0.39	0.57	0.35	*
4. Personnel/ Administration	0.28	0.43	0.21	*

Annual Sales ($1000s)	610.87	760.31	735.20	
Return on Assets (ROA)	17.88	11.90	14.09	*
Age of Firm	11.88	13.40	30.09	*

Note: The items marked with asterisks are significantly different across the modes.

reporting. The time-frame for planning is medium overall, but longest in matters relating to capital projects planning. SUs hire trained professionals most often in the accounting and finance area, followed by production. These firms are also significantly younger, have the smallest annual sales, and employ a larger workforce than the family firms. The workforce is smaller than that of BOs. They are significantly more profitable than the others, with family firms being second and buy-outs third in profitability. Obviously, their formula for success seems to work well.

Buy-Outs

The top four business *objectives* of BOs are the same as for the start-up group, but growth of investment ranks fifth for this group, higher than for the other two groups. Owner satisfaction ranks lower for BOs than for SUs and FFs.

The three most important *strengths* of the firms are the same for BOs as for the two other groups and the order of importance is the same as well. But these firms consider location to be a more important strength than SUs do. Product pricing, however, is seen to be less of a strength in their eyes than for the other two categories.

Buy-outs primarily focus their business *strategies* on local markets but rate themselves at or below the competition on quality, product variety, and innovation. Their product mix also contains more complex products. Relative to competition they feel they have greater control over costs. Their rate of return is the lowest among the three groups. BOs stress local markets like SUs, but tend to sell more proprietary products like family firms. Their strategies thus seem to be a mix of those used by start-ups on the one hand and family firms on the other, and this may be inappropriate for the needs of their clientele; hence the low profits. Customers who patronize local businesses may not be looking for complex products, and buy-outs, while depending on local markets, fail to provide the right product mix.

BOs' goals, strengths, and strategies do not correspond. They rate their product quality and innovation lower than the competition's, yet hold quality and service to be their central goals and consider them to be their strong points. This result plus the fact that they earn significantly lower profits than SUs or FFs (even though the latter are smaller) raises questions about whether these buy-out businesses choose the "right" strategies for their goals and strengths.

Referring to their *management practices*, reporting is more formalized than in either SUs or FFs, but like the others, they use formal reporting to the greatest extent in the accounting and cash management areas. Their planning horizon is the longest among the three groups, and the difference is statistically significant in new product-market entry planning. They use trained staff significantly more than the others. But, as with the others, trained staff is hired most in accounting and production. Therefore their management practices are close to what we visualize them to be in Table 6.1. Yet their profits are weak, which shows that the strategies do not fit well with the mode of entry.

Family Firms

The owners of family firms rank the same three objectives at the top, but value owner satisfaction significantly higher than either SUs or BOs. FFs rate themselves high on the same strengths as the others, but perceive themselves to be significantly stronger on cost control and use of production capacity. Their sales are drawn from broad geographic markets, and they offer standardized, complex products. Their costs and prices are higher than the competition's and they rate their innovation and quality lower than the competition's. The family firms, being much older, apparently expand their markets to cover larger territories, and prefer to sell a narrow line of standardized but more complex products. Their reliance on more complex products requiring proprietary know-how means their costs are higher and they cannot frequently modify the existing ones or introduce wholly new products. Yet, they are able to earn good rates of return with this strategy, very likely because they are good at cost control. Family firms are able to move into wider markets, mainly because they are more established and thus have the necessary resources and experience. When they cover large markets, these family firms probably cater to a different type of clientele compared to SUs or BOs.

Their *management practices* are more conservative, with formalization being the lowest in almost all areas. The difference is, in fact, significant in respect of use of regular written reports in accounting and finance. Their planning horizon is shorter and hiring of trained staff is lower. We would assume that being much older than the others, family firms would rely extensively on written reporting, even though they may not typically conduct extensive planning or hire professional management personnel. But they are low in all areas. Yet profits of these firms are the second highest, and hence their informal practices do not adversely affect these results.

IMPLICATIONS

The goal hierarchies, key strengths of the firm, and the patterns in the use of formalized reporting across the different functional areas like accounting are strikingly similar in all three groups. For all three groups the top three goals are product excellence, profitability, and survival of the firm. Founder owners and the owners of family firms, however, seek personal satisfaction to a much greater degree than those operating buy-outs. Buyers-owners view their firms more as a business for profit. All of these small firms, however, recognize that quality and service are keys to survival in the marketplace. The high emphasis on profit and survival also shows that while they value the satisfaction of being an entrepreneur, they are quite pragmatic and pay close attention to the operations end of the business.

All three types of firms judge themselves to be strongest in the same three areas, namely, quality, customer service, and firm image, although start-ups rate themselves significantly stronger. These strengths are in line with their goal hierarchy. Yet, there are also some differences in their goals and strengths. Founders rate themselves stronger on innovativeness and employee productivity while family firms pride themselves on their ability to control manufacturing costs and efficient use of plant capacity. We would expect BOs to pay close attention to management processes and hence to rate themselves high on overall management competence. Family firms appear to be more confident about their management competence than BOs. As we pointed out before, their business strategies are somewhat different, but none of these distinctions reach statistically significant levels, suggesting that mode of entry into business in and of itself does not make entrepreneurs necessarily predisposed toward certain types of strategies.

There seems to be a good "fit" among the goals, strengths, and strategies of these firms. For instance, SUs consider themselves strong on innovation and product quality, while family firms are rated significantly higher on cost control and efficient use of production capacity. These strengths match well with the product-market strategies used by these firms. This means that these two groups of firms know which areas are crucial for implementing their strategies well, and they are good at building strengths in these areas. There is not a clear match for the buy-outs. They perceive strengths in quality, service, and image, yet they rate their product quality and innovation below that of competitors. And judging by the comparative results on profitability, we can say that consistency between the strategies and the strengths of the firm is essential for success.

Management practices and systems are surprisingly similar across all three groups of firms. Particularly noticeable is the similarity in the relative order in which they use some of these systems. In all three groups, written reporting, long-range planning, and employment of trained staff are used to the greatest extent in the accounting-finance, second in production, third in marketing-sales function, and least in personnel. Evidently they all subscribe to the same philosophy about installing systems and procedures. They use procedures in those areas where the need is obvious; otherwise they are managed rather informally. All of them recognize the need for regular monitoring and long-range planning most in the accounting and cash management areas, next in production-related areas like capital facilities, and so on. This pattern is consistent with theory on how systems and procedures evolve in organizations. Management functions like production and finance tend to be systematized the most and the earliest because, as organizations' operations grow bigger and more complex, it becomes increasingly difficult to keep track of things without the aid of formal and regular reporting. The production area similarly needs to be systematized to ensure coordination among purchasing, manufacturing, shipping, and so on.

Checking for differences across the three groups, it is notable that business strategies do not vary with the owner's mode of entry. Rather, they are determined by factors like the nature of competition, type of industry, the general economic conditions in the region, and the firms' strengths and weaknesses.

They sharply differ in one area of management practice, that is, hiring of trained personnel for managing finances, production, sales, and administration. Buy-outs hire professional staff to the greatest extent in all these areas, showing that they believe these will help improve firm performance. Yet the fact that their rate of return is the lowest makes it doubtful whether these practices are helpful in and of themselves. More likely, firm performance depends primarily on the business strategies, and if these are inappropriate for the markets and customers, sophisticated systems do not help much.

Early in this chapter we raised the question of whether the entrepreneur's mode of entry had any impact on the way the firm was managed. The answer is both yes and no. Yes, because typically, firms managed by their founders tend to be younger and earn higher returns. They give more importance to some goals than buy-outs or family firms' owners-managers do, and most of their management practices tend to be informal. The answer is also no because, first, the most highly rated goals and key strengths are similar for all firms and their business strategies are not significantly different. All in all, these firms believe that success comes from providing a quality product to the customer, but the buy-outs seem to run into difficulties in translating this into reality.

There are basically two strategies: one route is taken by the founders' firms, namely, providing a broad product mix made up of simple products and catering to purely local markets. The second is the family firms' strategy of covering broad markets with more sophisticated products of acceptable quality. The mixed strategy of offering sophisticated products to local markets does not help buy-outs much. Further, the start-ups rely more on product quality, variety, and innovation than either FFs or BOs, showing that when individuals create new businesses they prefer to take the route of offering distinctive products and services. This supports the popular belief that innovation is the best route for entrepreneurs creating new ventures.

What do we make of the fact that some systems are substantially different, while business strategies are not? This implies that entrepreneurs approach choices on product-market strategies differently compared to how they choose management systems and procedures.

Business strategies vary with market conditions, while companies develop and design systems based on their beliefs regarding the right ways of managing.

How "entrepreneurial" are they? In Stevenson's paradigm,[21] more entrepreneurial individuals are "promoters." They are driven to product and market innovation, and take pride in their superior quality. Typically these managers prefer a flat, flexible, and informal structure to a rigid and hierarchical one and seek hands-on involvement in all matters. These persons may be apprehensive that systems and procedures reduce personal control and organizational flexibility. As we said before, SUs emphasize quality and innovation more than the others, but not to any uniquely greater degree. Further, both SUs and FFs have more informal and personalized methods of managing compared to buy-out firms. And this holds true even when these firms are quite mature. More important, their profit performance does not decline when they continue to run things informally. Part of the reason definitely lies in the small size of their operations. Both FFs and SUs generally employ a total workforce below twenty. Therefore, lines of communications are open. Their staff carries all the necessary information in their heads, and management can consult with personnel readily and respond to events quickly. Thus they can continue to manage in a personalized fashion. When firms do not grow rapidly by severalfold in sales or workforce, and instead grow at a slow pace, management may not find it imperative to install sophisticated procedures. BOs are uniformly more formalized in reporting and planning and hire more trained management personnel in all the functions. This is partly due to the fact that they are larger, and partly because the buyer-entrepreneur takes a less personal and more "rational" approach to business. The more complex operations of BOs perhaps require more extensive reporting and skilled staff.

All in all, to the extent that we associate informal, personal styles of management with a desire for flexibility, we could say that start-ups are more "entrepreneurial" than buy-outs. The relatively high degree of similarity in goals, organizational strengths, and management practices, however, makes it difficult to find any identifiable patterns of "entrepreneurial" management and associate them with specific modes of entry.

Although our survey was not geared to finding out specifically about owner-manager entrepreneurial behavior, when we interviewed some of these owners-managers, they had clear goals in mind. They were gutsy and highly persistent. This was true of start-ups as well as some of the managers of family firms. One case was that of the woman entrepreneur who started a transportation service for handicapped children. The impetus came from her inability to find adequate transportation for her daughter. Several banks turned her down for financing, and it took patience and mostly her own savings to slowly lease the buses and start the service. After several years of losses, the business was finally breaking even. Profit was clearly not the motive. This woman evidently was driven by the idea of an unmet need and hence an opportunity, and it was her faith in herself that kept her going. Similarly entrepreneurial was the decision style of the owner of a family-owned printing firm who decided to turn from bulk printing to specialty and graphics printing. He took a major risk in moving into unknown markets, and change in production technology demanded a heavy capital commitment. The owner-manager was not deterred by the gamble, since he was convinced that this shift was necessary for the future growth and profitability of the firm.

In conclusion, there are important differences in strategic management among SUs, BOs, and FFs, indicating that differences in mode of entry are likely to lead to differences in strategic management. Start-up firms and family firms remain more informal, and there is likely to be a better fit among their strategies, goals, and strengths. Buy-outs, on the other hand, need to reconsider their strategic approaches, recognizing that more systematic planning or reporting will not automatically improve performance. Yet, on the whole, these distinctions should be considered to be more in the nature of degree rather than of kind.

NOTES

1. J. A. Katz, "Entry Strategies of the Self-Employed: Individual Level Characteristics and Organizational Outcomes," in *Frontiers of Entrepreneurship Research* (Wellesley, Mass.: Babson College, 1984): pp. 396–408; W. B. Gartner, T. R. Mitchell, and K. H. Vesper, "A Taxonomy of New Business

Ventures," *Journal of Business Venturing* 4 (1989): 169–86; W. R. Sandberg, *New Venture Performance: The Role of Strategy and Industry Structure* (Lexington, Mass.: Lexington Books, 1986); K. H. Vesper, *New Venture Strategies* (Englewood Cliffs, N.J.: Prentice-Hall, 1980).

2. M. E. Porter, *Competitive Strategy* (New York: Free, 1980).

3. Z. Block and I. MacMillan, "Growing Concern: Milestones for Successful Venture Planning," *Harvard Business Review* 63 (Sept.–Oct. 1985): 163–67; N. C. Churchill and V. Lewis, "The Five Stages of Small Business Growth," *Harvard Business Review* 61/3 (1983): 30–41; W. B. Gartner, "Problems in Business Startup: The Relationships among Entrepreneurial Skills and Problems Identification for Different Types of Ventures," in *Frontiers of Entrepreneurship Research* (Wellesley, Mass.: Babson College, 1984), pp. 496–512; R. K. Kazanjian, "Relation of Dominant Problems to Stages of Growth in Technology-based New Ventures," *Academy of Management Journal* 31/2 (1988): 257–79.

4. Kazanjian, "Dominant Problems."

5. Marion Asnes, "The Empress of Ice Cream," *Vogue* (Dec. 1985): 158, 160.

6. Paul and Sarah Edwards, "Success Rate for Start-ups Improves," *Home Office Computing* (Feb. 1989): 40–41.

7. J. G. Burch, *Entrepreneurship* (New York: Wiley, 1986); Gartner, "Problems in Business Startup"; Gartner et al., "Taxonomy of New Business Ventures"; Vesper, *New Venture Strategies*.

8. Vesper, *New Venture Strategies*, 235.

9. Gartner, "Problems in Business Startups."

10. Bob D. Gibson, "A Gamble That Paid Off," *Nation's Business* (Jan. 1989): 38.

11. David J. Jefferson, "Corporate Experience Bolsters Small Firm in Big Ways," *Wall Street Journal* (May 22, 1990): B2.

12. "The New Nepotism: Why Dynasties Are Making a Comeback," *Business Week* (Apr. 4, 1988): 106–9.

13. Ibid., p. 107.

14. Steve Huntley and Jeanne Thornton, "The Silent Strength of Family Businesses," *U.S. News and World Report* (Apr. 1983): 47–49.

15. R. Beckhard and W. G. Dyer, "Managing Continuity in the Family-owned Business," *Organizational Dynamics* (Summer 1983): 5–12; H. Levinson, "Conflicts That Plague Family Businesses," *Harvard Business Review* (Mar.–Apr. 1971): 90–98; P. Davis, "Realizing the Potential of Family Business," *Organizational Dynamics* (Summer 1983): 47–56; T. Goldwasser, *Family Pride: Profiles of Five of America's Best Run Family Businesses* (New York: Dodd, Mead, 1986); J. L. Ward, *Keeping the Family Business Healthy* (San Francisco: Jossey-Bass, 1987).

16. "The New Nepotism," pp. 106–9.

17. Brett Duvall Fromson, "Keeping It All in the Family," *Fortune* (Sept. 25, 1989): 86–91.

18. J. H. Astrachan, "Family Firm and Community Culture," *Family Business Review* 1/2: (Summer 1988): 165–89.

19. H. H. Stevenson, M. J. Roberts, and H. I. Grousbeck, *New Business Ventures and the Entrepreneur* (Homewood, Ill.: Irwin, 1985), p. 4.

20. Churchill and Lewis, "Five Stages."

21. Stevenson, et al., *New Business Ventures*.

7

Organizational Life Stage
and the Small Business

Woods, Inc., a lumber company in the Mid-Atlantic region, is about 150 years old. It operates in a relatively mature and stable industry. The third-generation owner-manager of the enterprise, whom we interviewed, calls the firm a super senior citizen in the industry. He has this to say about the problems and concerns of his aging small business:

> Having survived for three generations, our firm has accumulated vitality that comes with the new generation owner-manager and the financial strength of the senior firm. There is a large sense of history, and we have a tendency to take a longer-term viewpoint than a company that is only 3 or 4 years old. We deal with almost everyone in our environment very differently . . . but as the company grows older it becomes more important for it to survive. It becomes almost a challenge to see how long the firm can be kept going within the family. The owner-manager of a senior firm is like the guy with a pie plate on the stick. I saw this happening in my own company when my father was managing it.

In contrast, Tech-Printing, Inc., a commercial printing company in the same region, has, ever since its inception in 1940, been riding on the technology wave of the printing industry. The third-generation owner-manager of the company, whom we interviewed, has this to say about the problems and prospects of this firm:

> After all that growth that we have experienced, we got to the point where we have five plants and the next largest market that we might have entered was in the Dallas–Fort Worth area. It is a region that is geographically so diverse and covers such a large area, that we thought that it is tough for a printer of our size to do the bulk of the work in the region. To open a plant in that area meant that the plant will be far away from our other facilities. We also felt that we could not capture enough market there to be really comfortable. . . . The other thing that has happened is that the sophistication in managing the business has changed quite a bit. No longer can one person, like my father, be the one to have dominant control of the company. The company is too large. . . . The technology in our business is moving at such a fast rate that my father no longer wants to understand it. We find it necessary to depend on a number of individuals for our success—individuals who do not own a piece of the company. As a family, we are learning to adapt to the new way of managing our business.

These are just two examples the demonstrate that in every organization a variety of developments occur independent of its will or the business strategies it follows.

In reviewing the strategies and performance of these and several other small businesses, we will use the age of the firm to determine its life stage. Age encompasses a variety of characteristics, such as size, diversity, and complexity. The experiences of the firms that we studied suggest that age affects small business strategies and performance in a variety of ways:

- New and relatively young firms possess a certain ideological "novelty," that is, a belief widely shared among members of the firm that the basic ideal of the business they are engaged in, its purpose, and what it has to offer the market and society at large are all new. It gives the firm drive, energy, and enthusiasm for all involved in the venture. With the passage of time, however, this novelty wears out.

- "Senior citizens" of industry, regardless of their size, grow more slowly than the "juniors."
- Owners-managers live and learn. Over time they see similarities in recurring events and decisions and tend to bureaucratize their enterprises. Over time their personal and family conditions change, and entrepreneurial burnout can occur.

This is not to suggest that the effect of age are unavoidable or that owners-managers cannot do much about them. Organizational management and product-management strategies must be continually tuned and retuned to deal with changes in life stage. In this context, two questions that owners-managers should ask themselves are:

- As my firm grows old and enters its next life stage, what kinds of changes should I expect and be prepared for in my business?
- What business strategies would best suit my firm at its present life stage?

The experiences of small businesses we have studied have led us to distinguish three life stages: juniors (firms one to nine years of age), middle-aged firms (ten to twenty-one years of age), and senior citizens (twenty-two years or older).

ORGANIZATIONAL EVOLUTION

The stages of small business growth and development have been described in the literature. Analysts tend to use the variants of pre-start-up, start-up, early growth, and later growth phases to describe the evolution of businesses. All the models suggest one thing: the business strategies and the degree to which each of them affects business performance depend on where a given organization is in the course of its evolution. Approaches that spell success at the inception stage may not be appropriate at the growth stage. For example, at the inception stage, a strength of most small businesses is know-how. In later stages of development, as businesses face competition and problems of growth, their organizational and managerial strengths determine success. Firms that are weak in those respects are forced to play defensively or quit the arena. In many organizations the evolution is smooth. Some organizations go through the changes abruptly, placing a strain on various parts of the company. Most firms, in real life, develop through a series of evolutionary and crisis stages.

Most successful small businesspeople, however, do not simply accept the life stage of their firms as given or uncontrollable. At times small businesspeople strive to change the evolutionary course of their firms, and at other times they react to and adapt to the life stage. This flexibility—a general willingness to be a prospector sometimes and a reactor at other times—is the key characteristic of the most successful small businesspeople. These people also correctly judge the beginning and end of each stage of life for their firms and the appropriate times for changes in their business strategies. The turnaround in the strategic orientation of Tech Printing illustrates the point.

In the late 1940s the adoption of the offset printing process revolutionized the entire printing industry. It brought in a new technology and a new manufacturing process. It was oriented toward running a lot of short-run work and resulted in lower initial costs and shorter preparation time. Tech Printing moved into the offset lithography field sooner than many of the other printing companies in the area. As a result of that move, the company determined to some extent the way the competition evolved in the region and the subsequent growth witnessed by the firm and its relative position in the competitive arena. In early 1980, reacting to a general decline in the government printing market, a slowdown in the economy, and intense price competition in the industry, the company backed off from its expansion strategy to consolidate operations at a few centers near the home base.

CHANGES AND THE SMALL BUSINESS

Changes in Business Objectives

Profit is an important objective to small businesses in all age groups. Successful owners act as their own venture capitalists, seeking profit and scrutinizing their decisions like venture capitalists would. A number of secondary objectives, however, may be instrumental in accomplishing the profit goal change over time. Survival of the business is on the minds of more owners-managers of junior and senior firms than of middle-aged businesses. Among juniors, the concern is to survive today to be able to see tomorrow's profits. So they tend to approach small business management with a "here and now" attitude, which is reflected throughout the firm. As the company ages, survival becomes an all-consuming concern and takes on a new meaning. The dominant focus tends to be "What do we have to do to survive, and how will we do it?" The way these questions are resolved determines the performance of the firm in its subsequent years.

Also, more middle-aged firms than juniors or seniors view market share, a measure of market dominance, as an important objective. It takes time for a firm to profitably pursue the goal of enhancing its market share. It is important to be certain that the firm is not at risk before it attempts to capture a higher market share. A larger market share per se does not mean high profits. A number of small businesses do not recognize that they can make a lot of profit on a small sales volume, although small volume does not carry with it the prestige that is often associated with larger sales. A number of strategies that do not emphasize market share may be particularly appropriate for juniors and seniors.

Changes in Owner-Manager Satisfaction

Owners-managers of young firms have great expectations and are brimming full of that "can-do" feeling. These qualities are essential for success. But when faced with hard realities and performance statistics, these individuals are easily frustrated and dissatisfied. Therefore, it is not surprising that the number of owners-managers reporting satisfaction is smallest in the junior group and largest in the senior group of firms (see Table 7.1). Owner-manager dissatisfaction readily permeates the firm and begins to take its toll on business performance. The owner could be the biggest handicap that a firm has! To avoid the risks and the associated frustrations, juniors must approach small business opportunities with modest and very clear expectations.

Table 7.1
Changes in Small Companies as a Result of Changes in Life Stage

Changes	Junior Firms	Middle-Aged Firms	Senior Firms
Importance of:			
Market share	23.4%	41.3%	32.2%
Survival of business	66.3	33.3	58.0
Owner-manager is personally satisfied with venture	91.9	98.3	100.0
Strength of firm is in:			
Cash management	42.9	58.8	42.0
Productivity of employees	47.9	39.6	38.7
Performance of firm is constrained by:			
Working capital shortage	55.1	49.2	48.4
Production capacity of plant and machinery	54.0	33.3	48.4

Note: Only statistically significant results are presented.

Changes in Organizational Strengths and Weaknesses

Many small business owners will testify to the fact that cash management is one area of business that needs constant personal attention. As shown in Table 7.1, junior firms do not have outstanding strengths in this area. Our findings show that weakness in cash management spills over into other areas of management. It prevents the firm from fully utilizing plant and machinery and achieving higher levels of performance. In general, this weakness reduces economic slack in the firm and limits the strategic options of owners-managers. The problems related to cash flow are less frequent in middle-aged firms. This is evidence of the level of maturity that usually occurs in this group. Relatively well-managed senior firms are very strong in finance, but some specific precautions are still necessary. Owners-managers of senior firms, particularly those who have seen the Great Depression, tend to take out of the business just what is needed to live on and leave the rest in the company. That is not always easy with the Internal Revenue regulations, but some owners believe that the larger the cash reserves of the company the better off their firms are. Although this viewpoint is valid to some extent, management of cash is a very important task and it is necessary to draw on all organizational resources to perform it well. It is particularly critical for juniors and seniors to institutionalize management practices that strengthen cash management. These firms can also formulate strategies that minimize the impact of a weakness in cash management, but at best this is a band-aid solution and the weakness will eventually catch up with the enterprise if it is not corrected.

Productivity of the employees of junior firms is very high. This is a distinct asset of juniors. Managers of new and relatively young firms generally are more enthusiastic than their counterparts in middle-aged and senior firms. This comes from the novelty of the enterprise and a widely shared optimism among all employees of the firm that they have a lot to achieve.

As time passes and operations are routinized, the novelty wears off. The tendency to say, "We tried this before and it didn't work," discourages the managers of senior firms from adopting new and innovative business initiatives. The firms routinize their operations to the point that they grow very rigid. More often than not seniors are identified in the market with a certain product and it is hard to break out of this image.

In part, the decline in productivity over time could also be attributed to entrepreneurial burnout. Owners-managers should prepare to arrest the impact of burnout by taking a leave of absence, attending a training program, bringing a new family member into the business, or inviting a new executive, who can challenge some of the current practices, to join the company.

Changes in Firm Characteristics

As one might expect, a number of physical characteristics distinguish junior, middle-aged, and senior firms (see Table 7.2). Most notably,

Table 7.2
Physical Changes in Small Companies as a Result of Changes in Life Stage

Changes	Junior Firms	Middle-Aged Firms	Senior Firms
Size			
Number of employees	15	40	36
Dollar sales ($1000s)	485	910	758
Complexity			
Relative breadth of product line	2.7	2.8	2.6

Note: Only statistically significant results are presented.

size (as measured by the number of employees and dollar sales) varies among the groups. On the average, juniors are the smallest and middle-aged firms are the largest. The senior citizens are not as large as middle-aged firms, indicating that some downsizing occurs after middle age. Owners-managers must be prepared to deal with this decline.

Even the most experienced owners-managers have difficulty adjusting to the changes in size that usually occur in their firms. They tend to view their businesses as single-plant, single-product companies, and they act accordingly.

As the company grows in size, the owner can no longer be the sole person responsible for planning. Planning has to become more of a group effort and requires team management. Owners-managers should strive to make other people responsible for decisions. They must understand what owners are striving to accomplish and what their game plan is. Inability or unwillingness on the part of owners to share their visions with others in their organization, who do not own a part of the company, could limit the rate of growth of the firm. Growth and evolution take a lot of getting used to, and successful owners-managers adapt their managerial thinking, leadership style, and administrative practices to fit the changing organization.

Interestingly, junior, middle-aged, and senior firms are not distinguishable on any of the measures of business complexity, that is, breadth of product line, number of manufacturing plants, geographical diversity of markets, and number of customers. As small businesses grow and prosper, their sales and the number of employees increase, but the firms retain their ''simple and flexible'' structure and focus on a few products, customers, and geographical markets. The approach of Woods, Inc., as stated by its owner-manager in a personal interview, supports this conclusion:

> Throughout the life of the firm, the organizational structure was flexible enough that different people did different things at any given point in time. During the 1950s, when our firm was both a wholesaler and retailer, our vice-president mainly dealt with internal problems—scheduling, payroll, shipping, purchasing. Purchasing is a particularly important function in our lumber business, especially when we treated it as a commodity. A small saving in purchase price can make a big difference to our bottom line. During the 1960s the same executive would devote all his time to selling, marketing, and servicing the customers. Organizational structure has been altered to accommodate power relationships between the professional manager and the owner-manager and entry of a new member of family into the business. But in all cases, emphasis was on retaining a measure of flexibility.

Changes in Performance

On a performance totem pole, middle-aged firms rank very high, followed by seniors; at the bottom of the totem pole are juniors. Industry sales conditions have different effects on firms on different age groups. Senior firms outperform all others in declining industries, while middle-aged firms hold the leading position in stagnant and growing industries. In all cases, juniors show the lowest profit. Regardless of size (measured by number of employees), the profitability of middle-aged and senior firms tends to be least affected by industry sales conditions. Being young is not always an advantage. Young firms are new in the competitive arena. Owners-managers lack experience in running an independent business; the firms have very limited resources; and these companies have not yet established themselves in the marketplace. As firms age, they develop ways of shielding themselves from environmental changes that could be threatening.

In industries that are plagued by frequent business cycles, one criterion seems appropriate: At the end of every downcycle in business, a firm should be a little larger than it was before the recession set in, as inevitably the firm gives back some of its gains during the downcycle. This consideration is particularly important in businesses (such as lumber) that are frequently hit by business cycles. During a recession almost all businesses follow the same strategies: Turn down the heat and turn off lights, lay off a few office employees, and so on. What distinguishes the winners and losers during a recession is that winners have a likely recession built into their growth strategies and, therefore, are better prepared to battle the slump. To quote from a personal interview with the owner-manager of Woods, Inc.:

> We survived several recessions, held our ground almost every time, and always did better than our rivals because we always played, whether there is recession or not, a defender type of strategy—keep our costs low, carefully manage the cash flow, and defend our firm from the onslaught of the larger rivals.

Prudent small businesspeople balance the opportunities of growth and the risk of losing all or almost all of the growth during a downturn.

IMPLICATIONS

Winners and losers can be found in all age groups. What, then, are the most profitable business strategies for firms in each age group? Experiences of the firms that we have studied suggest the following guidelines.

Organizational Management Strategies

Juniors stand to gain the most from careful advertising and promotions. Expenditures in both of these areas are growth- and expansion-oriented. Successful small firms tend to plan these activities on a short-term basis—about six to twelve months ahead. The results of these efforts tend to lag behind the expenditures, and the lags must be figured in planning the activities.

In a multigenerational firm, prospects for growth are very much dependent on the chances of the current owner-manager being succeeded by the next generation. Therefore, every growth opportunity must be assessed against one simple criterion: Growth that is likely to continue beyond the life span of the current management must be sustainable by the succeeding generation. If that is not possible, the growth strategy will be wasted. Whether a firm chooses to exercise its options of growth depends on the age of the owner-manager and the chances that he or she will be succeeded by another member of the family.

Seeking external assistance in the matter of taxation is very common in small firms in all age categories. In fact, according to our findings, there is no other aspect of business where help is sought by so many small enterprises. Juniors are the heaviest users of this help. Their primary goal in seeking external assistance is to get the most out of the complex array of tax incentives available to new and young small businesses. Other reasons why juniors seek advice on taxation are a general lack of experience in managing an independent business, a lack of familiarity with legal and regulatory aspects of the business environment, and the lack of resources within the firm to guide the owners in taxation matters.

Relatively profitable juniors assemble a management team that can handle production, selling, and administrative tasks. This is not to suggest that each of the tasks is performed by a specialist. But the firm must be capable of resolving the technical, marketing, and administrative problems that plague so many new and young firms.

A rather delicate issue faced by a family that owns a rapidly growing enterprise is the nature of the relationship between the family member who newly joins the firm and the "outsider" professional manager who has been with the firm for a number of years.

Invariably, relationships between professional managers and owners-managers are difficult. The smaller the company and the greater the age difference between the new owner-manager and the professional manager, the more difficult is the relationship. The inexperience and the youth of the succeeding owner heighten the conflict. In companies that are growing rapidly, the problem may not be that severe. So the anticipated growth of the firm should be a factor in recruiting a high-powered professional manager from outside.

Among middle-aged firms, careful monitoring of cash flow, manufacturing cost, and labor productivity are important for profitability. These practices, collectively, determine the operational efficiency of the firm.

The objective of the middle-aged firm in seeking external assistance should be to sustain the momentum it has gained by lining up finances, identifying new markets for products, and minimizing disruptions due to a lack of inventories or labor-management problems. The variety and the specific kinds of help sought by the middle-aged firm are symptomatic of the problems that generally plague this group and the complex array of factors that determine performance of the firms.

In the case of seniors, the organizational management practices that distinguish winners and losers are fine tuning the organizational structure, focusing on controlling accounts receivables and product quality, and careful planning of inventories. The firms in this category generally are very light users of external assistance. They tend to rely on in-house expertise to solve their problems. Rather long experience could very well justify this practice. But again, these firms run the risk of repeating their past mistakes and not realizing that the world out there is very different.

Product-Market Strategies

Turning to the product-market strategies that are effective in each age group, we find that the profitability of the junior firm is affected by the image of the firm, the breadth of the product line, and the percentage of total sales made by the firm in the local markets (generally the markets situated within one hundred miles). But product quality and percentage of total sales made directly to customers lower the performance of these firms. For juniors, product and market strategies enhance the firm's image. Attempts to push product quality to the point that it exceeds or equals the standards adhered to by the leading competitors could be damaging to profit outlook. It is only natural for a new and young firm to take pride in the quality of its products and services, but a high-quality offering may not sell in large enough quantities to earn an acceptable profit level. A sense of balance between product quality and firm image is essential for juniors.

During the early stages of a firm's development, the owner-manager's priorities should be to master the technology of the product or service and understand the marketplace. Most successful owners run lean, mean shops. They emphasize volume and work toward reaching the break-even point as soon as possible. During the early years of development, owners-managers are better off not being selective about the market segment they serve or the niche that the firm fits into. Development of strategies to identify niches and defend them from competitive onslaught should be deferred until such time as the firm is financially sound. As the firm grows, however, the management selectively enters new product and geographical markets. A new and small organization benefits from concentrating on a highly compact geographical market situated close to the plant and offering a wide range of product alternatives through intermediaries, such as agents. This approach gives the organization economies of scale and helps it face the challenge of growth while avoiding the problems of organizational coordination that are often associated with regional and national markets and direct distribution.

For middle-aged firms, company image is a significant determinant of performance. These firms cannot afford not to introduce new products or modify the old ones. Relying primarily on patents or trade secrets can restrict the firm's ability to bring out innovative offerings and thus reduces profitability. Charging prices above those of competitors also reduces profitability. These firms have been in business long enough to break out of the resource poverty that most junior firms experience. They are now able to roll down their prices in order to stay competitive and foot the bill for developing new and modified products.

When small businesses diversify into new or related products, they are best advised to avoid direct competition with larger rivals. In the 1960s, for example, Woods, Inc. launched laminated beams. This was a high-profit, low-volume item sold directly to contractors and builders. The major competitors in the field were the largest lumber companies in the world. They cut prices deeply to clear their inventories. Small businesses cannot match such cuts. Very soon management realized that the product line was not lucrative and withdrew from the market. Large organizations tend to have more staying power than smaller ones and can easily drive them out of business.

Most customers have a very long memory and do not forget poor business practices. A new, emerging firm can ill afford the wrath of its customers.

Focusing on local markets particularly helps the profit picture of seniors. Emphasizing product-related patents, trade secrets, or a highly standardized produce line, however, tends to restrict the strategic mobility of the firm. Also, manufacturing cost inefficiencies and a failure on the part of a senior firm to sort out its technical problems and to be competitive on costs can prove to be very expensive.

In general, the importance of local markets for small business profitability points to the need to select the location of a plant with extreme care. As noted previously, most small firms do not develop by multiplying the number of plants, nor can they relocate easily. Therefore, a long-term view of market opportunities should be considered when the initial site is selected. Ideally, the firm should be situated near its major markets. Of course, following a highly localized market strategy makes small firms particularly vulnerable to local business cycles. This risk should not be overlooked.

In sum, there is a relationship between the life stage of a small business, as defined by its age, and performance, as measured by the return on investment. We have reviewed a number of changes that occur in firms as a result of the changes in life stage and identified the strategies that are likely to be effective at each stage. This review is useful to every owner-manager in preparing for changes, assessing their impact on profit, and formulating and implementing effective strategies.

NOTE

A large portion of this chapter is reprinted from *Handbook of Business Strategy 1985/1986 Yearbook*, by William D. Guth, with permission of Warren, Gorham & Lamont Inc. Copyright © 1985. All rights reserved.

8

The Family Firm

The family business. For some people, the term conjures up images of the television show, "The Waltons"—a warm, supportive environment where John Boy and his dad, building furniture in the family barn, seem to end each workday with a hug and expansive smiles of self-satisfaction. For other people, the term connotes an environment characterized by bickering, jealousy, and petty tyranny from which there seems no escape. Not unlike a bad marriage, a family business can be an ongoing nightmare. How can owners-managers create a positive business climate, not only for themselves, but for future generations as well?

A large part of the answer is realizing how deceptively complex the task of business perpetuation can be. In the most simple terms, an entrepreneur starts a business that becomes successful, and later is joined by offspring who learn the mechanics of the business under their parent's tutelage. Eventually, when the parent entrepreneur succumbs to age, illness, or death, the successor generation takes over and continues the business. One parent, typical of many family business owners, summed up this approach with, "I just don't see what's so complicated about the whole thing. I started a successful business, and my kids are making a good living off of it. When I'm gone, the whole thing will be theirs, and while I'm sure there are going to be some problems, I know my kids love each other, and I trust they'll be able to work out their differences."

It is probably because this viewpoint is fairly typical that family businesses exhibit such a high mortality rate. According to one estimate, 65 percent of family businesses fail to make the transition between the first and second generation, while 85 percent fail to survive the second generation of owners-managers.[1] And while the elementary approach to continuing the business may be appealing because of its simplicity, it obviously neglects some very salient questions about the differences in motives, values, and abilities among family members. For example, what if there are two siblings in the business? How does the parent choose which child will lead the business into the next generation? And how does the family deal with the disappointment and possible resentment of the child who has been passed over? What about the problem of dealing equitably with a child employed in the business and another who has chosen a different career? If the parent's estate consists primarily of the family business, does the business get bequeathed entirely to the child in the family business, or is it somehow divided between the two? And if it is divided, how is the insider child's interest in business growth and reinvestment reconciled with the outsider's desire for dividends and liquidity? Obviously, the list of questions could go on indefinitely, but it is clear that the laissez-faire approach to business perpetuation relies perhaps more on luck and ignorant bliss than anything else.

At this opposite end of the family business perpetuation attempts is an approach that focuses quite heavily on the psychological makeup of the family members and the nature of the interaction between them. The underlying assumption of this approach is that before you can have a healthy family business, it is a pretty good idea to start with a psychologically healthy family. While the strength of the family therapy approach to perpetuating the business is its comprehensiveness, it is also one of its weaknesses. Because it generally requires consultants who are experienced in both business and family therapy, it is expensive. Due to its comprehensive approach, it can also be time-consuming. Furthermore, pragmatic entrepreneurs may see little value in the psychological exploration that this approach employs, and may actively resist any process that exposes their own shortcomings, either as a businessperson or a parent. While it is clearly appropriate, and even required, in some situations, the family therapy approach may be an unnecessary luxury for the majority of family-owned businesses.

Until recently, the owner-manager of an independent business had little factual guidance when it came to matters of business continuity planning. Certainly, there were professionals in law, accounting, and insurance who could provide technical advice, but quite often, there was little attention given to the more interpersonal issues of continuity planning. In the past ten years, there has been an explosion of advice in the form of books, business magazine articles, and seminars, yet it is difficult to determine the validity of the advice proffered. While many of these articles were written by consultants with extensive experience in the family business field, most of the illustrations consisted of a limited number of case studies. Thus, an interested owner-manager had little way of knowing whether succession was really a terrible problem that troubled most family businesses or whether only the worst cases reached authors, and therefore, was representative of only a small percentage of the family business population. The research described in this chapter is only part of the growing trend of empirical investigation to determine the validity of some of the relationships that have been offered in the prescriptive literature.

PLANNING FOR PERPETUATION

Fortunately, there is a middle ground approach for the business owner seeking to preserve the family ownership of the business. By focusing on a few critical areas of perpetuation effort, the chances of successful intergenerational transfer can be vastly improved. In examining the planning practices of a number of family firms, we looked at the extent to which they accomplished five specific perpetuation tasks. These tasks have often been mentioned in the family business literature as basic requirements of the continuation effort. The list should not be considered as a comprehensive checklist of tasks to ensure business perpetuation, but rather the absolute minimum that a responsible business owner should undertake. In other words, completing these tasks does not mean your business will survive longer, but not completing them will certainly diminish any chances for perpetuation. The five are:

1. A current will that accurately reflects the owner's wishes
2. A realistic valuation of the business

3. Enough "keyman" life insurance to fund buy-sell agreements or stock redemption plans

4. A formally designated successor to the current owner-manager

5. Effective communication of the owner's plan to family and key business associates

   Businesses that have relative success in completing these tasks will be referred to as "planners," while low-scoring firms will be categorized as "non-planners." It is important to note that we cannot make the same distinction between "successful" and "unsuccessful" firms that has been made in previous chapters, since success here would be the perpetuation of the business that may occur many years in the future. Furthermore, the research here is descriptive rather than prescriptive. It is probably safe to assume that the "planners" are better prepared to perpetuate their business than the "nonplanners." Indeed, one of the benefits reported by the planning firms is a much higher degree of confidence in the continuation of their business than reported by nonplanners. So while it may not be possible to state that practice X will definitely lead to business perpetuation," owners-managers who have done practice X believe that it will lead to a positive outcome. And the descriptive nature of the study can accentuate some traps that might befall the unwary. It should be noted that while the general assumption is that the continuation of th family business is desirable, there is no reason to believe that continuing the business within the family is important to all owners-managers. Forty-eight percent of the respondents we talked to indicated that continuity of the business in their family was either "desirable" or "highly desirable," while 26 percent rated family continuity as "undesirable" or "highly undesirable." Owners-managers who had founded their businesses tended to see continuity in the family as less desirable than those owners-managers who had either purchased or inherited their business. The degree of confidence that the owners-managers expressed in continuity was varied. When asked to rate their confidence that their business could continue with the same level of performance if the owner-manager were to die or be disabled tomorrow, 33 percent of the respondents indicated a "high" or "very high" degree of confidence, while almost 40 percent stated their confidence level was "low" or "very low." Those owners who had higher levels of continuity planning exhibited more confidence in continuity than owners-managers with lower levels. As one owner-manager said, "I don't plan on dying tomorrow, but I know that my financial house is in order. I've made my decisions and told the family. I can honestly say that if the business doesn't continue, it won't be because of anything I've neglected."

Business Size

Of all the organizational factors that may be related to business continuation planning, it seems likely that the size of the business, as measured by sales, net worth, or number of employees, would be one of the major considerations. A larger business may possess a number of advantages, such as excess resources or more sophisticated advisors, not available to the smaller firm. There is a cost in mounting a continuation planning effort, both in terms of professional fees and in the time investment of the owner-manager. The founder of one company said, "I've been through the legal and accounting routine before, and each time I ended up with thousands of dollars in professional fees, and end up with a good plan only to see the tax laws change three years later. I can either run my business or plan for all the estate stuff, but I just don't have the time to do both." For the smaller business, these costs may not be judged worthwhile. As the owner-manager of a smaller company put it, "This has been a good little business for me. It has supported my family and put the kids through college, but it really didn't have the sexiness to attract the kids, and I'm not sure that the potential was there anyway." This owner of a low performer was satisfied with the income produced and had a limited number of alternative career choices, but he realized that the business was not worth a major continuity effort.

The size of the business also affects the way potential successors view the firm. It may be difficult to attract potential successors to a smaller business. Unlike medieval times when a child basically had to take the trade of the father since there were very few alternatives, young people now have an almost unlimited variety of career alternatives. And the more capable and industrious the offspring, the more career alternatives are open. Thus, the family firm has to compete for its family successors with the biggest of the Fortune-500. All too often, the family business that is perceived as too small or as lacking in potential is passed over by the next generation of family members.

In one study of small business liquidations it was found that smaller companies were regarded as too personally demanding on the owner-manager. In a similar vein, Sue Birley found that potential family business successors were attracted by the possibility of exercising general management authority rather than performing all of the nonglamorous jobs associated with the very small firm.[2] As one potential heir to a very small family business put it, "I spent four years studying business at a good college and it is hard for me to see myself emptying the trash cans every night." The larger the company, however, the more likely it is to be an important financial asset to the owner-manager. And because of its size, one would expect that the owner(s) could afford the level of professional advice and the time commitment necessary for a major continuation effort. Research results indicate, however, that operators of larger businesses were no more likely to be planners, in the business continuation sense, than their smaller counterparts. This finding has troubling implications for heirs, employees, and even local communities. While the owners-managers of smaller companies may have good reasons for not planning for the continuity of their businesses (the companies may be marginal performers or may be too small to attract successors), the owners-managers of larger companies may be risking serious financial losses by not planning for the continuity of their business. It does not appear that the lack of continuity planning is restricted to "mom and pop" types of businesses.

Strategic Planning

If one examines the literature on management practices in smaller firms, the one ubiquitous criticism encountered is the lack of planning in smaller firms—not only in the sense of business continuation, but in the area of general business operations as well. The most frequent criticism, and one acknowledged by most owners-managers, is that the continuing press of day-to-day problems absorbs most of their time and there is really no opportunity to assess where the firm stands presently and what actions need to be taken for future success. This problem is exemplified by one company CEO who said, "I would love to think about what I need to be doing to make my firm more profitable next year, but two of my people in shipping didn't show up today, and I have a big order scheduled to go out tomorrow. What do you think I'm going to spend today working on?"

The fundamental assumption underlying this criticism is that firms that plan for the future tend to perform better than firms that do not. While the research results on this topic are somewhat mixed, the preponderance of evidence suggests that planning is generally accepted as a good thing to do. Examining the suggested smaller company planning processes reveals a spectrum of practices that run from rudimentary to very sophisticated. In the most elementary form, planning consists of determining where the firm is now, where it should be at some point in the future, and what actions are required to effect the desired change. This focus on the future state of the firm will generally lead to some consideration of the factors comprising the business perpetuation efforts. After all, while much of the future may be unknowable, the aging and the eventual retirement or death of the current owner-manager is one certainty that can be planned on. Who will own the business? Who will manage the business? How will the estate taxes be paid? Because many of these perpetuation issues are intrinsic to the strategic planning effort, it is expected that smaller companies that practice some form of strategic planning will also engage in planning for the perpetuation of the business. One would then expect to see a "planning orientation" that addresses both general strategic issues and business continuity issues in the planning process.

Forty-three percent of the responding firms were classified in the lowest level of strategic planning (SLO), while fifteen firms (26%) were classified as high strategic planners (SL4). It was expected that firms that engaged in higher levels of strategic planning would also engage in higher levels of business continuity planning, and the results indicated that such was the case.

While there are certainly differences in the focus of strategic and continuity planning, there is enough overlap in areas such as mission statements, financial investment policies, management development practices, and the like that a discussion of a strategic plan will soon lead to the longer-term future of the business. It appears that John L. Ward's suggestion that "the intricate overlay of family and business plans requires that the family not separate strategic business planning from family planning" is an accurate description of the planning process in these firms.[3]

Perceived Family Harmony

A central theme in almost any newspaper article about family businesses concerns the concept of family harmony. Typically in these accounts, the family is portrayed as a group of bickering individuals, unable to resolve their conflicts. There seems to be no end to these tales of family disintegration. For example, the patriarch of the Bingham publishing empire in Kentucky dismantled the family business when his son and daughter started a public feud that racked both the family and the community. An even more outlandish story is that of the Shoen family of the U-Haul Company. The founder of U-Haul gave much of his stock to his children, only to be later thrown out of his own firm by his son. Amid lawsuits, counter-suits, and even charges of one son punching his stepmother, U-Haul gradually lost its first-place position in the retail rental market. While stories about disharmony in family businesses can rival anything found in the supermarket tabloids, there are firms such as Stew Leonards' in Connecticut or the R. F. Johnson Company that should make us remember that family conflict and family businesses do not have to be synonymous.

Perceived family harmony is an exceedingly complex concept. For example, the level of harmony may differ depending on whether one is looking at inter- or intragenerational relationships. Likewise, the absence of vigorous debate and disagreement may indicate an apparent high level of harmony, but, in actuality, mask a set of relationships where conflict and rivalries are merely submerged. Finally, there is the question of whose perception of harmony is being examined. Many senior generation owners-managers may simply be oblivious to or severely underestimate the degree of conflict extant in their organization and family.

Resolving many of these questions was beyond the scope of our research. Instead, we were concerned with the level of family harmony perceived by the current owner-manager and its relationship with the level of business continuation planning. A family business characterized by a high degree of harmony among family members is one of the most valued work environments, and continuity of such a business is likely to be important to family members, irrespective of financial performance. Likewise, the literature cites family businesses in which relationships are very poor, and the termination of these businesses may be the most desirable outcome.

Not surprisingly, high degrees of family harmony and high levels of continuation planning go hand in hand. As with many of the other results, alternative arguments regarding causality can be presented. On the one hand, a high degree of harmony in the family business may make the continuity planning process a more tolerable task, and the harmonious relationships may reinforce the importance of continuity planning in the owner-manager's mind. Alternatively, it is also possible that the planning effort serves to clarify ambiguous relationships and problems, thus serving to increase the level of harmony in the business. Some suggest that the cost of maintaining family harmony may be high in that new ideas and challenges are suppressed in the interest of family harmony. Our research does not address this issue. Quite possibly the harmony associated with the business continuity planning reported in this chapter resulted in continuity plans that are far less than optimal. The planning process itself, however, may be the best method of ensuring that pertinent issues are addressed and harmony is still maintained.

Board Composition

While planning for business continuity may be a prudent step, not only for ensuring the business's survival but also for conserving the family's assets, many owners-managers do not view it as a pleasant task. One sixty-three-year-old owner-manager described the dilemma: "I know I should be turning over the reins, but I've been running this place for thirty-two years. I wouldn't know what to do with myself if I wasn't doing this job tomorrow. I know my son wants to run the company, but it doesn't seem like too much to ask for him to wait a few more years until I'm gone."

If continuity planning is not an altogether enjoyable job, what makes an owner-manager undertake this task? One possible answer is the urging, or the assistance, of an outsider, but an outsider in the family firm context usually means a professional, such as an accountant, lawyer, or banker, who depends on the continuing goodwill of the owner-manger for a continued relationship. Such a relationship is not always conducive to independent counsel.

One obvious distinction between the typical family business and its publicly owned counterpart is the separation of ownership and management control. The public company is managed by professional managers, who are guided and advised by a board of directors elected by the stockholders. In the family-owned business, the top manager is usually the sole or majority owner, and as such, possesses much of the same power as a feudal prince. As long as no laws are broken, the owner-manager can either maximize profits or play golf. In effect, there is no oversight, direction, or guidance supplied by any group. While this lack of oversight may not be a limitation in most circumstances, it may allow the owner-manager to escape or defer unpleasant duties.

Firms scoring high in business perpetuation used their boards of directors more than did nonplanners, and those boards were more likely to contain a high percentage of nonfamily members and nonemployees. Yet only in rare cases did the board assume an adversarial posture with the CEO. One owner-manager said of his relation with his board, "They probably pushed me a little more than I like about my estate plans, but they (the board) had built up so much credibility with me on other business decisions, I really had no choice than to go along with their wishes."

This sentiment reflects some of the key qualities of board members mentioned by CEOs. First, the board members must have the respect of the CEO in terms of business judgment. Personal or family friends are often not viewed as having sufficient business experience to make material contributions. Second, board members, while independent, must possess empathy for the chief executive. An understanding of the CEO's problems is a prerequisite for membership. Finally, board members need a regular and ongoing relationship with the firm. Planners' boards meet almost twice as often as nonplanners, and generally discuss matters of importance. This quality probably diminishes the utility of accountants, lawyers, or other professionals whose contact with the firm may tend to be sporadic.

The Owner-Manager's Age

Given the certainty of aging and eventual death, the age of the owner-manger is an important factor in continuity planning. The need for succession planning is not typically noted until the owner-manager enters the later stages of life. If the owner-manager is relatively young, the perceived need for continuity planning may be minimal. But as the owner-manager ages and friends and business colleagues succumb to various ailments, the idea of one's own mortality and the need to plan for one's replacement becomes far more salient.

While it seems likely that older owners-managers would engage in higher levels of business continuity planning in anticipation of death or retirement, owners-managers regularly deceive themselves regarding their own mortality. While it may seem far-fetched that the older business owner would not be prepared for passing on the business, consider the following statement from one of the business owners in our sample: "My father lived a healthy and active life until he dropped dead at eighty-two. I'm only in my early sixties and I figure I've got a good ten to fifteen years left."

For the firms included in our research, there was no significant relationship between the age of the current owner-manager and the extent of continuation planning. This lack of planning as the owner-manager ages confirms the viewpoint that many owners-managers ignore the increasing probability of their death and the effect it will have on their organization.[4] The lack of continuation planning has especially ominous implications for successor generations in many family firms. Heirs and potential successors are likely to be disappointed if they expect the current owner-manager to begin planning for continuity at "the appropriate time." For many owners-managers "the appropriate time" will be forever in the future.

The CEO's Locus of Control

Another personal characteristic that may influence planning for business continuity is the psychological concept of locus of control.

Individuals who possess a highly internal locus of control tend to believe that they, rather than outside forces, control their fate. Subjects with an external locus of control orientation tend to view their condition as a result of luck, chance, fate, or the influence of powerful others. It has been shown that CEOs with an internal locus of control orientation tended to implement innovative and proactive policies in small firms.[5] For family firms, two alternative and opposing arguments can be made in regard to locus of control. The more traditional argument would be that highly internal owners-managers would be proactive and advocate continuity planning since their involvement would largely dictate the immediate future of the business. Frequently cited factors such as the fear of death, fear of loss of control, and loss of self-esteem, however, may alter this relationship in the family business context. Internal owners-managers, when faced with these negative outcomes, may choose to maintain control indefinitely and avoid any continuity planning. Likewise, those who show a highly internal orientation may believe that aging and death are largely under their control.

Our results indicate that internals are more likely to engage in higher levels of business continuity planning than are externals. There is no significant difference in locus of control scores between founders and nonfounders. Since the alternative to continuity planning is to do nothing, the failure to plan effectively removes the current owner-manager from influencing the future of the business. Several respondents who had done little or no continuity planning stated that they could not anticipate all of the contingencies that might occur after their death and, therefore, had to rely on the goodwill of their survivors.

The relationship of locus of control and business continuity planning has a number of implications for the family business owner. First, it may be possible for outsiders to evaluate an owner-manager's predisposition toward business continuity planning. An owner-manager who exhibits an external orientation may be reluctant to initiate the planning process and may require more assistance and urging than someone with an internal orientation. Stakeholders, such as family members and employees, may want to make such an appraisal to determine their risk exposure before investing their funds and their lives in the family business.

Second, a person's locus of control orientation is not completely fixed. A study of small business owners after a natural disaster had destroyed their businesses showed a very high external score. After a period of physical rebuilding and organizational development programs, these same owners' orientation had shifted to being more internal, that is, they believed they were more in control of their own fate.[6] This instability in locus of control orientation suggests that there may be certain periods in life when people may be more receptive to the idea of continuation planning. Interested parties such as family and employees should seize these opportunities when presented. Likewise, if it is mandatory that continuation planning be undertaken when the owner-manager is in a predominantly external orientation, then those types of organizational development programs that result in a shift toward the internal may be helpful.

IMPLICATIONS

The findings of research reported in this chapter confirm many of the generally held conceptions regarding family businesses, but there are at least three major implications for practitioners that bear attention.

First, the lack of planning, in both the business strategy and the business continuity areas, should not be considered to be an isolated case study or a spectacular "horror story." Twenty-five of the fifty-eight responding firms were classified as engaging in no strategic planning whatsoever, and, in terms of business continuity planning, twenty-four of the responding owners-managers did not even have a will that accurately reflected their current wishes. Owners-managers could gain a long-term strategic advantage over close competitors merely by having a well-conceived will.

The second implication is that while a will represents one of the most fundamental tools in the business continuity effort, it is often harder to address the more personal issues of designating a successor and communicating the continuation plan to affected parties. The scores of the five factors used in the scale indicate that the interpersonal areas of actually designating a successor and communicating the continuity plan to interested parties are accomplished less successfully than wills, valuation, and the like. While a will and a valuation may be important elements of continuity planning, these tools only represent the senior generation's wishes. The acts of selecting, developing, and communicating with successors are the actions that continue a business, not merely dividing assets.

Third, the high degree of correspondence between strategic and continuity planning suggests that efforts in the strategic planning area may pay dividends in the continuity planning area as well. Since strategic planning is not a concept restricted to family business, it benefits from the increased legitimacy of what some call the "outsider" perspective. It is less emotionally charged than a question like "What's going to happen to the business when Dad dies?" Thus, it may be easier for family businesses to approach continuity planning via the strategic planning process rather than tackling it directly as a family issue.

Almost anyone with recurring exposure to family businesses can relate horror stories about the lack of continuity planning in this type of firm. The consequences can range from mild, in the case of a successful business that gets a incompetent successor and drifts slowly into competitive decline, to tragic, as when a family feud erupts over the future of the business and the family itself is split asunder. Retrospectively, it seems that many of these negative consequences could have been avoided with a minimal amount of planning effort. What, then, needs to change?

First, current owners-managers must recognize that the responsibility for continuity planning is primarily theirs. While others may try to push or influence, the owner-manager can either facilitate or stimy the process. An objection that is often raised by nonplanning owners-managers is, "How can I plan when I don't know whether the family is interested in (or capable of) keeping the business or whether it will be sold after my death?" While this question certainly affects the continuity planning effort, its importance in the context of the rudimentary jobs outlined above is often overemphasized. The tasks of drawing a will, allocating assets, and providing for estate liquidity are not unique to the family firm. Anyone with a substantial estate faces the same job. The tasks of selecting and training a successor, as well as communicating the plan to family and employees, are singular to the family firm, and these tasks should add value to the business whether it is kept in the family or eventually sold. What many business owners lose sight of is that while current income may be depressed by investing in the next generation of managers, the overall market value of the business is increased.

Second, the notion that continuity planning is the sole prerogative of the owner-manager needs to be recognized for the fallacy it is. While it may be true that the owner-manager should control the content of continuity planning, the other stakeholders in the family and in the business have a right to know that the required planning has taken place. Spouses should know that they will not be called upon to operate a business that they have only heard about over the dinner table. Children need to know that the family business they have decided to join will not be liquidated to pay estate taxes. Employees need to know that the company they work for will still be in business the day after the founder's funeral.

The concept of continuity planning as an obligation requires both sensitivity and persistence on the part of the family, employees, and professional advisors. Offspring in the family business may be concerned about their occupational future, but resist pressing the continuity planning issue for fear of appearing greedy. Planning for the conclusion of a career, or even one's life, is difficult for most people.

Some pundits labeled the 1980s "the decade of the entrepreneur," and the act of founding a business was raised to folk hero status. Perhaps we need to change our focus somewhat and accord more respect to the "business concluder" as well as the business founder. While there may not be as much glamor attached to putting one's affairs in order at the end of a career, we need to start viewing it as an obligation attached to owning a business.

Third, the owner-manager needs to utilize the resources that are increasingly available to the family firm. There is a growing body of academic research that specifically addresses the problems of family business continuation. There are more articles in the popular business press about family business issues. There are a mushrooming number of consultants specializing in family business issues who can bring expertise to bear that is well outside the capability of most family firms. All of these resources can make the overwhelming complexity of continuity planning somewhat less overwhelming.

NOTES

1. David Ambrose, "Transfer of the Family-Owned Business," *Journal of Small Business Management* 21/1 (1983): 49–56.

2. Ibid. See also Sue Birley, "Succession in the Family Firm: The Inheritor's View," *Journal of Small Business Management* 21 (1986): 36–43.

3. John L. Ward, *Keeping the Family Business Healthy* (San Francisco: Jossey-Bass, 1987), p. 99.

4. Leon Danco, *Beyond Survival* (Cleveland: Center for Family Business, University Press, 1975).

5. D. Miller, M. F. R. Kets de Vries, and J. M. Toulouse, "Top Executive Locus of Control and Its Relation to Strategy Making, Structure, and Environment," *Academy of Management Journal* 25 (1982): 237–53.

6. D. F. Jennings and C. P. Zeithaml, "Locus of Control: A Review and Directions for Further Research," in *Proceedings, Academy of Management* (Dallas, Tex.: Academy of Management, 1983).

9

Women-Owned Enterprises

Statistics show that women are starting small businesses at twice the rate of men, and they account for 25 percent of all small businesses. Survival rates of women-owned enterprises compare favorably to those of male-owned ventures.[1] Apparently many women are successful as "entrepreneurs," that is, as owners-managers who take the risks of starting their own businesses and nursing them through the difficult years of early infancy. It is useful, therefore, to identify the strategies and management practices associated with successful women-owned enterprises (WOEs).

It is strongly debated in the literature whether the gender of the entrepreneur has an influence on the success of the enterprise. This chapter looks at the strategies, management practices, and leadership styles of successful women-owned enterprises. Our interest is in identifying the "fit" among seven strategic elements of women-owned businesses. To start with, we will look at what past literature says about how women entrepreneurs manage their businesses.

MODELS OF WOE STRATEGIC MANAGEMENT

The literature provides conflicting portraits of strategic management in women-owned enterprises. One stream of literature argues that there are several factors that are unique to women as managers.

Success or failure of women entrepreneurs is influenced by these unique factors. For instance, women enter business for different reasons than men, and their personality characteristics, strengths, and weaknesses as business leaders are different. Hence strategic management in WOEs will very likely be distinct. In contrast, others maintain that women managers behave in the same ways as male managers do, and therefore, women entrepreneurs manage their businesses like male entrepreneurs. These scholars argue that men and women face the same challenges, problems, and opportunities, and respond in similar ways.

Two contrasting models of strategic management in women-owned businesses can be derived from currents of thinking on women and leadership. These divergent models can be labeled the *feminine model* and the *entrepreneurial model*. The feminine model holds that women manage in different, "womanly" ways.[2] In contrast, the entrepreneurial model is derived from the notion that successful female entrepreneurs manage their ventures in much the same way that any typical successful entrepreneur would, and women-owned businesses fail for much the same reasons as a male entrpreneur's business. The salient features of these two models of management are summarized in Table 9.1.

The Feminine Model

This view is based on the negative experience of many women in corporate managerial positions. Corporate women often find themselves excluded from positions of authority and leadership—even today when they make up 40 percent of people in professional and managerial occupations.[3] The reasons are many. "They quit or deliberately leap off the fast track. They miss the children. They miss not having had children. A better opportunity comes along. . . . They also expected equal treatment in the workplace."[4] Often women seem to be still subject to the stereotype that they lack leadership qualities.[5] These notions have been shown to be invalid and may be slowly changing,[6] yet they are widely prevalent among male leaders in business, producing formidable institutional barriers to success. Such social and institutional obstacles plague women in all fields, hence success is equally difficult for women in the field of "entrepreneurship." They find it

Table 9.1
Models of Strategic Management in WOEs

THE FEMININE MODEL	THE ENTREPRENEURIAL MODEL
1. Shared Values	1. Shared Values
Modest goals for profit	Aggressive goals for profit
Primary interest in personal satisfaction	Interest in continuing growth
Prefers to remain small	Interest in profit greater than interest in personal satisfaction
2. Strategies	2. Strategies
Marketing: sells only products that need personalized service; enters and remains in small, local market niches	Marketing: markets diverse products; niche approach is used initially, but seeks large markets as business grows
Finance: enters low-capital business; able to invest only limited capital	Finance: relies on equity in the beginning, but borrows extensively with growth
3. Structures and Systems	3. Structures and Systems
Structure remains informal, decentralized, and small	Structure is informal but but centralized initially; more formal as firm expands
Motivation systems depend on personalized and nonmonetary rewards	Motivation systems use both monetary and nonmonetary rewards, but stress monetary incentives
Operations control remains weak, and systematic record is almost nonexistent	Operations control is weak at first, but systematic procedures are introduced with growth
4. Staff and Skills	4. Staff and Skills
Staff size remains small, not hire trained personnel or use expert advice	Staff size grows with businesses, will hire trained staff as firm expands
Prefers to hire female employees	Hires based on expertise or experience
Firm remains weak in management, particularly in finance and planning	Firm is initially weak in management skills, but acquires them with growth, beginning with finance and planning
5. Styles of Leadership	5. Styles of Leadership
Friendly, personalized, team-oriented, and informal style. Firm stays small to ensure employee satisfaction	Style is personal and informal but centralized at first. Grows more professionalized and delegative with expansion

Table 9.1 (Continued)

THE FEMININE MODEL	THE ENTREPRENEURIAL MODEL
Entrepreneur is low in assertiveness and sense of power	Entrepreneur is bold, decisive result-oriented, but caring
Intuitive and emotional approach to decisions	Decision making is intuitive initially, but more rational with growth
6. Performance	6. Performance
Profits and growth remain low	Profits and growth initially low but increase over time

more difficult, for instance, to obtain bank loans or to get suppliers to extend credit, because bankers and suppliers tend to place less faith in a women entrepreneur's management ability. In fact, success in business venturing is particularly difficult for women entrepreneurs compared to women in corporate careers because, in the case of male entrepreneurs, success has been much more difficult than for male managers.

There are several reasons behind this argument. For one thing, entrepreneurship is more demanding because it requires a strong need for achievement, self-confidence, internal locus of control (i.e., the belief that success or failure in an enterprise depends on your own efforts and resources rather than on luck or other outside forces), assertiveness, and risk-taking propensity to a much higher degree than a corporate career does. Second, it requires significant amounts of financial and other resources. Third, the entrepreneur needs to wield influence not only within the business, but with several important outside groups. Further, the risk of failure is very high, with only one among three new business ventures surviving beyond the first two years.[7]

In the face of such formidable barriers few women venture into starting a business of their own. Those few who do are found in female-dominated service businesses, and manage them in "womanly" ways. A few of these survive to remain small and marginally profitable. Women initiate businesses in sectors that are generally "accepted" as being appropriate for women's roles in society at large. They start enterprises in fields that are low-capital, service-oriented businesses like beauty salons, small grocery stores, gift shops, fabric shops, janitorial services, restaurants and delicatessens, child care services, nursing and dietician services, and some real estate agencies. Aggregate statistics on business support this thesis, since 75 percent of female-operated businesses tend to be in the retail and service categories. Also, in 1984, these women-owned businesses accounted for less than 15 percent of total business receipts in these sectors, indicating that most remain very small.

The feminine model holds that WOEs remain small and marginally profitable, and seldom outgrow the start-up phase, partly because the markets for the types of products and services they offer tend to be primarily local in scope, and partly because women entrepreneurs lack the vision and strategic and operating abilities needed for expanding them into large-sized businesses. They make up the majority of the "dwarfs" in the small business world. It is true that initially all enterprises start small and local and suffer from shortages of capital; but in the life cycle of most growing businesses, soon there is a turning point, when they achieve growing profits and are better able to secure financing and expand. The strategic orientation of successful entrepreneurs is to think bold and big for the long term, whereas the typical female entrepreneur continues to have a limited vision and think in terms of the short run.

In the feminine model of the WOE, women-owned enterprises are conservative and oriented toward survival rather than high growth or high profit. In fact, economic objectives for business rank well below such values as personal achievement and the satisfaction of "being one's own boss." Turning to strategies, in marketing they seek and remain in small local market niches, since the female entrepreneur prefers to be the service provider herself. Few of them can comfortably delegate these responsibilities and hence few can expand. Their financial strategy parallels this conservatism. They have experienced serious difficulty in establishing credit in the start-up phase, and continue to face perennial shortages of capital because they never really become financially sound. Hence WOEs adopt a cautious and risk-averse financial strategy.

Turning to their structures and systems, like all new ventures they start as informal and simple unstructured organizations. But the similarity soon ends because, unlike the aggressive and growing business venture, WOEs seldom outgrow this stage and move toward a formalized structure. Their management system also demonstrate the weaknesses of female entrepreneurs as strategic managers. Many women entrepreneurs are unsure of what information systems to use. Hence financial and operational monitoring is weak or nonexistent. This results in poor control and continued weakness in profitability and resource position. With regard to their staffing, they feel more comfortable hiring women even if male candidates are better equipped for the tasks. Also they tend to be averse to managing large workforces with trained staff and full time job assignments. Turning to the patterns in their management skills, the educational level of women entrepreneurs may be quite high but they tend to come from the liberal arts background, and hence their managerial skills are deficient. They find it particularly difficult to manage such matters as finance, business planning, and market analysis. In fact, many women entrepreneurs have often pointed to these as their areas of weakness.[8] Styles of leadership in WOEs are intuitive and emotional rather than rational, and more people-oriented than results-oriented. For example, they continue to do such simple tasks as answering all phone calls. Hence women entrepreneurs conduct business in distinctly "womanly" fashion.

The Entrepreneurial Model

This model is derived from the research that argues that the majority of leaders in business behave in similar ways. Studies have shown that self-concepts as well as leadership styles tend to be the same for male and female leaders in general. Both men and women see the "masculine" styles of decisiveness and goal orientation to be essential for a successful leader, and most leaders perceive themselves as having these characteristics.[9] A recent comparison of men and women who have made it to the top of the corporate career ladder showed that they give high ratings to some of the same prerequisites for success:

a strong track record in performance, being smart, and ability to manage subordinates. But their ratings differ for others. Women saw help from superiors, a strong desire to succeed, and ability to take career risks as very important, but men did not rate these as highly.[10]

Applying this reasoning to women running their own businesses, they would behave no differently than other entrepreneurs. After all, all entrepreneurs enter sectors that are open to them given their economic and family background, education, work experience, and so on. Women entrepreneurs are no exception. The majority of women-owned businesses are found in the low-capital, localized, personal services type businesses, but as more women enter new careers they gain the expertise and experience necessary for venturing into new sectors like high-tech businesses. Indeed, there are early indications that this may be happening. In 1987 roughly half of all professional and technical workers were women.[11] Even now significant numbers of female-operated businesses are to be found in such nontraditional fields as construction, manufacturing, communications, transportation and public utilities, finance, insurance, and real estate. Besides, it has been shown that male and female owners-managers of business have similar entrepreneurial personality profiles. They both show high levels of achievement motivation, persistence, aggressiveness, independence, goal orientation, self-confidence, and internal locus of control.[12]

The life cycles of business ventures and strategic management approaches in WOEs follow the same patterns found in all successful ventures. They start with few employees and limited resources and struggle to survive. The key questions they face at start-up are "Can we get enough customers, deliver enough products and services to become a viable business?"[13] As business survives the early infancy and becomes profitable, owners adopt more aggressive strategies, formal systems, and procedures. They start recruiting trained personnel for managing affairs in key areas like accounting, taxation, and sometimes, production and sales. There will be rudimentary specialization of tasks, with the trained personnel being primarily assigned to manage matters in their own areas. Later, some of these move into high gear on growth and expansion. Businesses at this stage begin to employ full-time trained staff to manage their routine operations.

Planning and budgeting become more crucial. Entrepreneurs increasingly disengage themselves from day-to-day affairs, concentrating more and more on planning for the long-term future of the business. Regular written reports become an important part of the management information system.[14]

In other words, WOEs follow the same prescriptions that any successful entrepreneur uses. As such, strategic profiles of successful women-owned ventures are typical of all successful ventures over their life cycle. They are small, cautious, and modestly profitable in the early stages; some grow into large businesses, depending on the environment, personal objectives, and background factors of the owners-managers.

If this holds true, then we should find examples of both the marginally profitable and the dynamic and high-growth ventures among WOEs. A recent survey of women-owned businesses uncovered twenty businesses that had over $100 million in annual sales, and sixty that had over $20 million.[15] Success in profits or growth in these businesses happens for the same reasons as for any typical new venture.

The new breed of female entrepreneur is aware that success needs hard-headed business skills and sets out to learn them and do things the right way. A coproprietor of a Manhattan clothing store for executive women puts it, "The trouble with most entrepreneurs (male and female alike) is that they have this great idea for a business, and they're so in love with that idea, that they're sure that everybody else will fall in love with it as soon as it hits the market—so they rush into the thing without the right kind of planning." Accounting, marketing, and planning were the skills that the first generation of women entrepreneurs acquired along the way, and the successful ones were fast learners. But she and her partner did not leave it to trial and error. Instead they honed the business skills that they learned in corporate careers getting ready to start their business. They spent three years planning for a business of their own and their scouting revealed that there was one vacant market niche with high potential, that is, clothing for executive women. After they settled on their enterprise, they played an elaborate game of "what if" in preparing their business plan to perfect all matters to the last detail, and demonstrate to suppliers, real estate agents, and bankers that they knew how to handle all contingencies.[16]

Some women business owners start without such systematic preparation and are content to earn a small profit. Mary Anne McFarland used to organize Christmas parties at the department store where she worked. They were such a hit that friends suggested she go into the party-planning business. When she circulated brochures about her business, she found that most people wanted only floral arrangements done for their parties, and preferred to do the hiring of the caterer and writing the invitations themselves. So she got into the Floral Boutique. She started with only $500 and her garage, but in the few years since her start-up she has managed reasonably well in spite of some expensive problems along the way such as when a basement flood ruined a large batch of flowers. For Mary Anne owning a business means two primary benefits—the opportunity to express her creativity and lack of pressure.[17]

CASE STUDIES

These stories and others show that there is a broad range of women entrepreneurs who can manage businesses in a variety of ways. There are examples of both ''feminine'' and ''entrepreneurial'' models of management.

As a first step in assessing how far the real-life profiles of the strategic management in successful WOEs correspond to the feminine or the entrepreneurial model, we interviewed five women entrepreneurs.[18] All of them have successfully survived the crises of the start-up phase and have at least reached the break-even point. These women started ventures in traditional as well as nontraditional sectors and were larger than a one-person operation.

Sandy's Real Estate

Until recently few women entered the real estate business. Sandy thus took an unusual step when she started her company in the mid-1980s to sell executive homes. A middle-aged married woman, she had seven years' experience as a successful real estate agent with another developer, but felt frustrated when her talents were not recognized and she was not made a partner. Also, she often wanted to do things her own way. With encouragement from a developer friend, she started her own agency with a contract to be the exclusive sales agent for his business. She used her personal savings of $20,000 to start the venture. Three years after start-up, she had generated substantial sales and they were growing rapidly. Profits started flowing and she was confident that her company would be even more profitable in the future. Like most new entrepreneurs she worked long hours with almost no pay, and at the time of the interview was still handling most of the big customers herself because she did not feel her firm was secure enough for her to delegate key sales and management issues. But unlike many start-up-stage women entrepreneurs, she felt that she had the business skills necessary to make her business grow. Her objectives were to earn high profits, achieve high growth, and be her own boss.

Her strategy was to focus on the one market niche she knew well, and use a personalized approach with prospective customers for selling homes. Another key strategy was to scout for and obtain contracts with developers. Her record keeping was simple, following the standard practices that she was familiar with through her past experience with real estate companies. Her staff consisted of three agents, including one coworker from her old firm, and her pay and compensation packages were highly competitive because she believed that she could offer better service than the competition through superior personnel. She saw herself as highly personal in her style, both with staff and customers.

Monique's Boutique

Monique quit her "dead-end" job of eighteen years at the local phone company and gave up her pension rights to open a nail boutique in a local shopping mall in southern New Jersey. Due to her inexperience, she did not check the market carefully initially. The mall closed soon after she opened. She checked the malls more carefully the second time. After running her boutique for three years, she started to earn enough for a comfortable living. In the next three years she opened three more stores and all stores were earning moderate profits. She did not have immediate plans to add more boutiques. She felt that the strategy of adding the nail business line to her beauty salon gave her an innovative niche in a generally declining business. According to her, the quality of her service was "no different from anyone else's" and she had no special philosophy about managing. She was able to get an SBA loan with her husband's cosignature, but later she was able to obtain bank credit. To begin she hired two people who had work experience in the beauty salon business, and as she expanded, she added five more people. A part-time person kept her books and an accountant did her taxes. Even though it had grown beyond being a one-person operation, her business remained informal and she saw no reason to change it. She herself did not have skills in the beauty business, and her goals were modest, being mainly to get away from a dead-end job and make a reasonable living.

Gina's Tanning Studio

Gina did not like being a housewife. She wanted to join her father's construction business, but he felt that a woman did not belong in that business. With a degree in mathematics and physical education, she tried a number of jobs: she was a high school teacher, a legal secretary, and a service manager at a car dealership. She then helped her boyfriend's construction business in advertising and computers. There she learned important business skills. She decided to get into a business of her own. She settled on the tanning studio idea after trying a friend's "sunbed" while on vacation. Realizing that this concept had not caught on in the northeastern United States, she became enthusiastic. Putting up her home as collateral, she raised the $25,000 needed to open a studio in suburban Philadelphia. The first six months were extremely discouraging and she lost heavily, but after more aggressive advertising, she started making enough to pay her bills. She became profitable after the first year and a half, and opened a second studio, which turned a profit in three months. She then got the idea of franchising her business. By the third year, she had two franchises and four studios of her own, and her loan was fully paid off. A local bank invited her to apply for a half-million-dollar expansion loan and this helped her open five more studios the following year. She conducted thorough marketing surveys to identify target markets. She was fully aware that her business was a high-risk business, both because of "the fad element" and because people often doubt the safety of the tanning process. She spent substantial amounts to "educate" the public. She made use of good business practices, such as using professional advertisers and conducting market surveys. Her college training made her good at keeping track of numbers. Her strategy of starting with an innovative "product" paid off well, and she was aggressively growth- and profit-oriented. She employed fifteen staff members, including a bookkeeper. Each of her studios was a separate unit in the organizational structure, run largely on its own with occasional supervision from her. She considered her management style to be personal and decisive, and her systems to be sound in sales, advertising, and accounting. She said her personnel have the right skills, as proven by the continued growth of her business.

The Marine Construction Services Company

Cathy had been a real estate agent for a number of years when she felt she needed to challenge herself more. She discovered that she really liked the business aspect of her real estate work. At this point she decided to get training in the marine construction services business, and then with a woman attorney friend started the marine services company. She prepared herself well for the venture by going through night school in business. Since her family was in the construction business, she could draw on their advice as well. But she did it all herself on a day-to-day basis. As she put it, "I think you have to have a certain kind of personality and attitude that you are going to be successful. A lot of people are not willing to put themselves on the line." Although financing was difficult at first, she does not think that this was because she was a woman. "Anyone with our (in)experience in the industry would have been treated the way I was. They wouldn't care who I was as long as the paper was right." But problems did occur with customers. "It was an advantage in one way being a woman, but just because they remember you it doesn't mean they will necessarily trust a woman in this type of business." She built a medium-sized business over the seven years she was in business, with fifty-eight employees, multimillion-dollar sales, and a strong rate of return. She and four vice-presidents ran the company. She herself was mainly involved in long-range planning and financial decisions, and kept in touch with important clients. She delegated much of the day-to-day work to her subordinates.

Ellen's Interiors

Ellen studied fashion design, retail management, and business in college. She worked for a while as an assistant to the treasurer in a local hospital, and then decided to start her own fashion and interior design business, which she did on a part-time basis for a few years. She then decided to go full-time into a training and production unit for decorative items. In training students for the next year and a half—some of whom she recruited for her staff—she looked for "people skills." "In decorating, we work very closely with our clients. We want their look in the room . . . not a stamped look." She was very supportive of her designers and her marketing stressed participation in community events like Welcome Wagon and free seminars to the community on interior design. She did not see department stores as her direct competition because "we do it on a more personal level." She planned to grow large enough in three years to go international—into Canada, France, West Germany, Australia, and Japan. Financial success was a key goal.

GENERAL OBSERVATIONS

Reasons for Entry

Some women are attracted to entrepreneurship because they feel that they will not be facing as many obstacles to success as they would face in a corporate career. Men (especially minorities and new immigrants) also start their own business because they feel that the usual routes to career advancement are closed to them. Actual and potential disenchantment with job opportunities are reasons for women to move into business. It may be dissatisfaction with a slow career, or a perception that entrepreneurship is a fast track to success, or a belief that conventional careers are closed due to such factors as age, education, or family status. Other women cite different reasons, such as the presence of an attractive business idea, the desire to be one's own boss, the desire to make it on their own and build something of their own, or monetary success. Thus, for the most part, women choose to become entrepreneurs for much the same reasons as men.[19]

Type of Business

There is a diversity among the businesses started by women, some being in the traditional, "female-dominated" service businesses, and others in nontraditional fields. Female entrepreneurs in traditional businesses do not feel they are competing with male-owned enterprises, whereas nontraditional entrepreneurs feel they have to continually prove themselves to be better than male competitors in order to build and keep clientele.

Objectives

The owners of Monique's Boutique and the Floral Boutique rated profit much lower than other goals like the desire to be their own boss or to give expression to their skills. For the others economic goals like income, revenue growth, competitive standing, and earnings were the prime objectives. Many women would like to see their firms become the best in their businesses. The construction firm was at least four times as large as the others and its owner viewed growth and building the firm into the best business of its kind to be a key objective, along with her interest in a personal challenge. All the women displayed tenacity and drive to keep working to make their businesses successful. The owners of the tanning studio and the nail boutique, for example, initially found capital very hard to come by and managed by dint of sheer determination, willing to pay themselves close to nothing.

Strategies

Interestingly, all of these businesses adopted some common strategies. Customer orientation, finding a viable niche, and establishing a credible market image appeared to be the key marketing strategies. They also emphasized superior customer service and innovative or unique products/services. They adopted a very personalized approach to service, taking care to ascertain and satisfy the particular requirements of each customer. Their financial strategies probably closely mirrored the entrepreneur's experience in obtaining credit. In the start-up phase they all had difficulty in procuring capital. This is confirmed by other observers of new ventures. They all had to manage very frugally, with the owner scrutinizing all expenses and keeping close control of finances. But most of them expected to grow and were quite willing to use credit as needs expanded.

Structures and Systems

As we noted before, only a few of our women entrepreneurs grew fast, but for these firms, the structure became more formalized, with subordinates handling the day-to-day tasks. The marine services firm (the largest) showed the typical functional structure with professional managers in charge of different functions like sales and service, accounting, and so on. But the others remained relatively small and the owner continued to help in customer service and purchasing. From the beginning, even the smaller firms in our interviews took care to maintain very simple but systematic procedures for record keeping on revenues and expenses. Other observers have also found that successful women entrepreneurs focus on maintaining close control of costs and sound cash position and good planning.

Staff and Skills

Many of the women took courses in areas like financial management and business planning, suggesting that while women entrepreneurs' backgrounds may not make them strong in business management skills, they (more than men?) tend to be willing to get training to fill the gaps. Those who were growth-oriented adopted systematic management practices even in the early phases of their ventures. They also reported approaching external sources of management and technical expertise such as government agencies and business associations.

Do they tend to hire more women employees? Yes, when the firm offers services that are typically provided by women. But in other firms the owners hire the best person for the job.

Styles

In describing their management styles, some come close to confirming that they adopt a distinctly "feminine" style of leadership. They often adopt a family approach to their employees. Some of them, in fact, did not want to grow too large for fear that they might lose the personal touch with either customers or employees. Even Cathy, who as the owner of a large firm used the personal style of management much less than the others and described herself as being goal-oriented, felt she was sensitive in her approach to her employees. "Men direct criticism at a person rather than a product. Women are lot less likely to say you're no good. Instead they say 'you made a mistake and this is it.'" But there was no leniency in work expectations. Interestingly, two entrepreneurs, the real estate firm owner and the beauty salon owner, even though their firms were quite young and small, asserted that they managed their firms in a highly results-oriented fashion. On the whole, the women entrepreneurs showed a high degree or concern for their employees, and preferred to involve them in decisions. Yet they made sure that they controlled the key decisions and were willing to be decisive. It is quite likely that management styles of female entrepreneurs may become more task-oriented as their businesses grow in size, yet female entrepreneurs do seem to prefer a more people-oriented and less autocratic style.

Performance

Monique's Boutique grew only marginally, but the others have grown well in sales and, to a lesser extent, in profits. Thus the record varies across the firms, except that they have all remained solvent financially—keeping in line with the high priority they gave to financial soundness. Conservatism was the norm in financial management and the growth objectives for several of the entrepreneurs were modest, but this seemed primarily to be a product of their concern that a big gamble might hurt the financial viability of the firm. The majority did not deliberately avoid high profits and growth, or attempt to remain small, as the stereotypical "feminine" model would have us believe. That many of them were growth-oriented was also clear from their observation that entry barriers were low in their businesses, and they had to actively work at keeping their competitive edge in service.

We draw these conclusions from the small number of in-depth interviews we conducted with women business owners. We cannot be sure that what we see from this small number of firms actually holds true for the many women-owned enterprises that are operating in the United States.

PROFITABLE STRATEGIES FOR WOMEN-OWNED ENTERPRISES

In order to study the strategic management patterns of WOEs on a much larger scale, we analyzed 163 women-owned businesses. The data give a broader picture than just looking at a few firms from up close.

We first split the 163 businesses into three groups: (1) those with a negative ROA, or incurred losses, during the last three years; (2) those that were moderately profitable (ROA in the range of 0–13 percent) during the preceding three years; and (3) firms with average ROA exceeding 13 percent. We analyzed the data several ways, results are presented in Table 9.2.

Relatively unprofitable firms (group 1) rated their top four objectives as product quality, market image, firm survival, and profitability. Obviously their hearts were in the right place, and they knew that profits and survival were vital, but these businesswomen somehow could not produce the profits. Why? These firms' strategies were to sell in local markets and they mostly sold directly to customers. They frequently modified products and services offered, and felt their costs as well as their productivity were lower than their competitors'. But they rated the quality of their products as better than their rivals'. Their reporting systems were informal, but compared to the high-profit firms, the losing firms paid slightly greater attention to long-term planning. Their use of professional staff was lower than in the moderately profitable firms, but was very similar to that in the high-profit group. Lastly, these entrepreneurs seemed to be more people-oriented in their management styles. Their workforce was smaller, and they were somewhat younger than the other two groups.

Table 9.2
Profitability of WOEs

Variables	Group 1	Group 2	Group 3	Comments
	Losing Firms	Moderate-Profit Firms	High-Profit Firms	
Objectives				
Profitability	4.86	4.64	4.72	Groups 1 & 2 are different
Revenue growth	4.71	4.67	4.49	
Market share	3.86	3.56	3.52	
Product quality	5.00	4.96	4.97	
Survival of firm	4.93	4.82	4.84	
Market image	5.00	4.91	4.91	Groups 1 & 2, Groups 1 & 3 are different
Personal satis-faction	4.64	4.47	4.72	Groups 2 & 3 are different
High living standard	4.23	3.59	3.77	Groups 1 & 2, Groups 1 & 3 are different
Strategies				
Percent in local sales	88.92	80.24	78.35	
Customization of products	1.62	1.57	1.62	
Frequency of product innovation	2.93	2.85	2.95	
Percent in direct sales	84.54	83.62	83.19	
Relative selling and promotion expenses	2.42	2.75	2.75	
Relative quality	4.17	4.15	4.41	
Relative price	2.83	2.87	3.01	
Relative production costs	3.00	3.19	2.98	

Table 9.2 (Continued)

Variables	Group 1 Losing Firms	Group 2 Moderate-Profit Firms	Group 3 High-Profit Firms	Comments
Relative labor costs	2.75	3.51	3.20	Groups 1 & 2, Groups 2 & 3 are different
Systems, Staff, Skills, and Styles				
Information reporting				
Finance	1.97	2.35	2.19	Groups 1 & 2 are different
Marketing	1.85	2.16	1.99	Groups 1 & 2 are different
Reporting				
Costs	2.08	2.20	1.96	Groups 2 & 3 are different
Time-Horizon for Planning				
Finance	5.23	5.53	5.09	Groups 2 & 3 are different
Marketing	3.69	4.04	3.81	
Personnel	4.36	4.43	4.27	
Use of Trained Staff				
Production	0.18	0.19	0.19	
Finance	0.29	0.31	0.28	
Marketing	0.21	0.32	0.26	
Personnel	0.21	0.17	0.18	
Leadership Style				
Consideration	56.43	52.89	50.83	Groups 1 & 3 are different
Task	41.14	40.47	42.07	
Age of Company	13.29	21.15	18.43	

The moderately profitable group of women entrepreneurs (group 2) stressed the objectives of product quality, market image, firm survival, and revenue growth. Their strategies were to seek sales from broader market, sell better-quality products and services, spend more on promotion, price the competition, and hire high-quality workers. They formalized their reporting systems and adopted a longer-term view in planning. They also hired trained staff for managing finance, sales, and production.

Looking at the general profile of high-profit firms (group 3), their top four objectives were the same as the others' except that these entrepreneurs considered personal satisfaction a key objective. Their strategies were to look for sales from broader markets, innovate more often than the competition, sell better-quality products at competitive prices, and achieve similar costs but higher sales productivity. Their systems were simpler than the medium-profit firms', and their planning horizons were shorter. They also employed trained personnel to a lesser extent than group 2. Like the other two groups, they had a higher rating on people-oriented style of leadership compared to the task-oriented style.

Apart from these overall impressions, what were the significant differences among these three groups?

Looking first at groups 1 and 2—the losing group versus the moderately profitable group—the losing group attached significantly greater value to the three objectives of profitability, market image of the firm, and providing a high living standard to the owner. On strategies, the profitable group's labor costs (rated relative to their key competitors' costs) were much higher than those of the losing group. Reporting was much more formalized in the profitable businesses. There were no significant differences in the other areas of systems or staff, and the leadership styles were also similar. The losing group had a significantly smaller workforce. Age differences were nonsignificant.

Groups 1 and 3—the losing versus the highly profitable businesses —differed significantly on the importance attached to the two objectives of market image of the firm and providing a high living standard for the owner. Both of these were more important for failing businesses. There were no significant differences in strategies, systems, or staff, but the entrepreneurs of highly profitable firms stressed the consideration style of leadership substantially less. The high-profit businesses were much larger.

The results can be interpreted as follows. The emphasis on market image and personal living standard objectives seems to be misplaced. This probably prevented these businesses from channeling their energies toward the right strategies. The right strategies would have been to stress paying higher wages to their personnel. It may seem odd that a higher labor cost means higher profit, but this can be explained easily. The more profitable firms strive to employ better-quality staff, which of course means they pay attractive wages. Interestingly, the losing firms used formalized reporting much more than the highly profitable ones, even though they were smaller in size. Since they were much smaller, these firms did not need regular formal reporting, and paying attention to these procedures very likely took away precious management time and resources from thinking about improving quality and service, and from focusing on growth. In fact, growth seems to be very critical for profit, because the losing firms were significantly smaller than the medium- and high-profit firms. And losing firms remained small. In other words, these firms were not smaller merely because they were younger. Rather, they did not wish to, or even if they did, they could not, grow. This is clear since the average ages of the firms in the three groups were not significantly different.

Having looked at the factors that hold back the losing ventures, the next question is: What are the strategic recipes of the high performers? The profiles of the more profitable WOEs were quite similar to those of the moderately profitable ones. Some exceptions were that the highly profitable women entrepreneurs attached greater importance to the personal satisfaction objective compared to those in group 2. In the matter of strategies, the medium group rated the productivity of their labor as being very similar to that of their competitors', but the high group rated their productivity as being above their competitors'. And the difference in scores was significant. Further, the medium group's scores on labor costs were significantly higher. Both of these results points to the same phenomenon, namely, that while profitable firms in general paid high wages, the productivity of labor was much higher in the highly profitable firms. They utilized their staff's skills much better. As far as systems, the highly profitable firms used regular written cost reporting much less, and financial planning was primarily short term-oriented. The size of their workforce (staff) was also much larger. There were no statistically significant differences in the leadership styles of these entrepreneurs, although the high-profit entrepreneurs scored slightly higher on results-oriented style of leadership compared to the medium-profit entrepreneurs. This suggests that when leaders are more results-oriented, they in fact take the steps to achieve strong results. One important step in this regard is to ensure that productive employees are hired as well as utilized. Surprisingly, high-profit firms used the least amount of written reporting on cost information, and we interpret this to mean that they had a more hands-on approach to cost control. Their shorter-term orientation in financial planning reinforces this reasoning, because this indicates that they planned budgets for the next few months very carefully.

Briefly, the keys to higher profits lay in cost vigilance and employee productivity. All the firms paid attention to matters like product quality, service, new product introduction, and the well-being of employees, but the more successful ones set themselves significantly apart by achieving high levels of productivity and concentrating on careful budgeting and planning for the next six months to one year.

Apart from the differences among the three groups, what can we say about the relative importance of objectives, strategies, and systems for profitability? The significant results, shown in Table 9.3, tell an interesting story.

Only one objective—market share—had a significant impact on profitability. Women entrepreneurs who paid more attention to increasing market share as an objective did worse than those who were less concerned about this. Evidently, this objective was inappropriate for the types of businesses these women were managing. Pursuing market share would mean trying to compete strongly with the rivals, and sometimes this meant battling with the larger, stronger rivals with more resources and market reputation. More often than not, such head-to-head competition hurt these small firms. This was due to the fact that firms tuned into this objective probably tended to enter the wrong markets and adopt the wrong strategies, systems, and so on. They should have looked for ways for growth, such as focusing on vacant or less competitive niches.

Table 9.3
Relative Effect of Objectives, Strategies, and Style on Profitability

Variable	Relative Effect (Beta)
Objectives	
Market share	-0.17
Strategies	
Relative product quality	0.25
Frequency of product innovation	0.32
Relative production costs	-0.42
Relative sales per employee	0.24
Percent of direct sales	-0.22
Relative price	0.24
Leadership Style	
Consideration style	-0.25

Note: Only statistically significant results are presented.

More profitable firms did not compete on price. These firms delivered innovative products of higher quality, and at the same time strove for cost efficiency and productivity. Indirect sales (selling through retailers) increased profits because sales could increase without incurring the costs of setting up added numbers of sales operations on their own. The positive beta for a large workforce signified that firms had to grow in size of operations in order to be able to earn higher profits.

Interestingly, few of the systematic management practices and procedures that so many textbooks prescribe had any impact on profitability. All in all, successful women entrepreneurs relied on their hands-on involvement and on their own judgement, rather than on systems and procedures like explicit advance planning or regular review of written reports. Nor did they extensively use trained staff. The rather contradictory findings are not as unsettling if we remember that we are dealing with organizations that are quite small. These small-scale enterprises did not need to set up elaborate systems and procedures. Typically the principal owners-managers were active day-to-day managers, and were well aware of what was going on. Therefore, they needed a system by which they could readily generate written reports when they needed them, rather than having to review them regularly. One other curious result was that, although all of the women entrepreneurs were high on the consideration style of leadership, a lesser emphasis on this people-oriented management style was evident among the more profitable businesses. This shows that while these women did show consideration to their employees' well-being, they also were also clearly results-oriented—very much in line with what we found in the one-on-one interviews.

IMPLICATIONS

First, many women-owned businesses are highly profitable and prosperous and do not remain marginally profitable and small. Further, it is clear that the profitable ones focus on certain distinct factors compared to the less profitable ones. Product quality, innovation, and efficiency are the secret behind their success. These strategies have worked well for many male-owned firms as well, and hence it seems that women-owned businesses use the same formulas as any typical successful enterprise. Today the majority of women-owned businesses may be in the "traditionally female" sectors like personal services, but that is mainly because in the past few women acquired the technical and managerial skills or work experience needed for starting any other types of businesses. In fact, even now many women in these "traditional" businesses have become highly profitable by using the same types of product-market strategies as male-owned enterprises.

Growth is critical to profitability. Businesses in the long run cannot remain viable without growth. Therefore, it is imperative that when they start their own business, entrepreneurs should carefully select and enter markets with attractive growth opportunities. Small firms can sometimes do well, even if the state of the national economy is depressed. What matters for these ventures is the state of the regional or local markets. Because they start from a small base, they can continue to grow without exhausting the sales potential in their markets or making inroads into the bigger competitor's markets. As we saw earlier, these firms are better off not aiming for market share. Often entrepreneurs start their businesses based on hunches and rarely undertake a market analysis. Yet they should not be carried away by a "great product idea" but thoroughly scrutinize market prospects before taking the plunge.

Contrary to the thesis that women might manage their businesses in "womanly" ways, these entrepreneurs demonstrated that they succeed by being results-oriented. They are quite concerned about their employees' well-being and are considerate of their needs, yet they judge them mainly on performance. They value motivated and competent employees and hence are willing to pay top dollar to get them and keep them. In contrast, many of the owners of losing businesses seem to pay insufficient attention to results. As regards management practices, this chapter offers a somewhat surprising result. WOEs do well without regularly using written reports to monitor operations, without adopting long-term planning, and without hiring trained staff. As we mentioned before, this is a consequence of the fact that, for most part, these businesses are very small, employing less than twenty part- and full-time employees, and this makes it possible for them to be run in highly informal ways. WOE owners-managers seem to do well as long as they know how to grow with a quality product and control their costs. They need to grow bigger before they find information systems and explicit advance planning indispensable.

NOTES

1. K. McDermott, "The 80s: Decade of Women Entrepreneurs," *Dun & Bradstreet Report* 33/4. (July–Aug. 1985): 14–16; U.S. Government Printing Office, *The State of Small Business: A Report to the President* (Washington, D.C., 1987).

2. D. D. Bowen and R. D. Hisrich, "The Female Entrepreneur: A Career Development Perspective," *Academy of Management Review* 11/2 (1986): 393–407; R. D. Hisrich and C. Brush, *The Woman Entrepreneur* (Lexington, Mass.: D. C. Heath, 1986).

3. "Why Women Aren't Getting to the Top," *Fortune* 108/8 (Apr. 16, 1985): 40–45; "Why Women Are Still Not Getting to the Top," *Fortune* 122/3 (July 3, 1990): 40–62; "The Glass Ceiling," in " The Corporate Woman: A Special Report," *Wall Street Journal* (Mar. 24, 1986); G. Powell, *Women and Men in Management* (Newbury Park, Calif.: SAGE, 1987).

4. "Why Women Aren't Getting to the Top," p. 40

5. B. Gilmer, *Industrial Psychology* (New York: McGraw-Hill, 1961); M. Horner, "Sex Differences in Achievement Motivation and Performance in Competitive and Non-competitive Situations" (Ph.D. diss., University of Michigan, 1968); R. M. Kanter, *Men and Women of the Corporation* (New York: Basic, 1977); V. F. Nieva and B. A. Gutek, *Women and Work: A Psychological Perspective* (New York: Praeger, 1981).

6. C. D. Sutton and K. K. Moore, "Executive women: Twenty Years Later," *Harvard Business Review* 63/5 (1985): 68–73.

7. H. Aldrich and E. R. Austen, "Even Dwarfs Started Small: Liabilities of Age and Size and Their Strategic Implications," B. Staw and L. L. Cummings, eds., *Research in Organizational Behavior* (New York: JAI, 1986), 8: 165–98; C. Borland, "Locus of Control, Need for Achievement and Entrepreneurship" (Ph.D. diss., University of Texas at Austin, 1975); J.A. Honraday and J. Abboud, "Characteristics of Successful Entrepreneurs," *Journal of Personnel Psychology* 24/2 (1974): 50–60; J. A. Timmons, with L. E. Smollen and A. L. Dingee, Jr., *New Venture Creation: A Guide to Entrepreneurship* (Homewood, Ill.: Irwin, 1985); K. H. Vesper, *New Venture Strategies* (Englewood Cliffs, N.J.: Prentice-Hall, 1980).

8. Hisrich and Brush, *Woman Entrepreneur*; M. A. Humphreys and J. McClung, "Women Entrepreneurs in Oklahoma," *Review of Regional Economics and Business* 6/2 (1981): 13–21; T. Mescon and G. E. Stevens, "Women as Entrepreneurs: A Preliminary Study of Female Realtors in Arizona," *Arizona Business* 19/7 (1982): 9–13; E. T. Pellegrino and B. L. Reece, "Perceived Formative and Operational Problems Encountered by Female Entrepreneurs in Retail and Service Firms," *Journal of Small Business Management* 29/7 (1982): 15–24.

9. K. M. Bartol, "The Sex Structuring of Organizations: A Search for Possible Causes," *Academy of Management Review* 3 (1978): 805–15; K. M. Bartol and M. S. Wortman, "Male versus Female Leaders: Effects on Perceived Leader Behavior and Satisfaction in a Hospital," *Personnel Psychology* 28 (1975): 533–47; J. B. Miner, "Motivation to Manage among Men and Women: Studies of Business Manager and Educational Administrators," *Journal of Vocational Behavior* 5 (1974): 197–208; G. N. Powell and D. A. Butterfield, "The 'Good Manager': Masculine or Androgynous?" *Academy of Management Journal* 22/2 (1979): 395–403; G. N. Powell and D. A. Butterfield, "The 'Good Manager': Does Androgyny Fare Better in the 1980s?" *Academy of Management Meetings*, Chicago, 1986; R. M. Stogdill, O. S. Goode, and D. R. Day, "New Leader Behavior Description Subscales," *Journal of Psychology* 54 (1962): 259–69.

10. A. P. Morrison, R. P. White, and E. Van Velsor, *Breaking the Glass Ceiling* (Reading, Mass.: Addison-Wesley, 1987).

11. Powell, *Women & Men in Management*.

12. F. W. Waddell, "Factors Affecting Choice, Satisfaction, and Success in the Female Self-employed," *Journal of Vocational Behavior* 23 (1983): 294–304; J. F. De Carlo and P. R. Lyons, "A Comparison of Selected Personal Characteristics of Minority and Non-minority Female Entrepreneurs," *Journal of Small Business Management* 17/4 (1979): 22–29; J. Demarest, "Women Minding Their Own Businesses: A Pilot Study of Independent Business and Professional Women and Their Enterprises. (Ph.D. diss., University of Colorado at Boulder, 1977); D. L. Sexton and N. Bowman-Upton, "Female and Male Entrepreneurs: Psychological Characteristics and Their Role in Gender-related Discrimination," *Journal of Business Venturing* 5/1 (Jan. 1990): 29–36.

13. N. C. Churchill and V. L. Lewis, "The Five Stages of Small Business Growth," *Harvard Business Review* 61/3 (1983): 32.

14. Ibid.; N. R. Smith and J. B. Miner, "Type of Entrepreneur, Type of Firm, and Managerial Motivation: Implications for Organizational Life-cycle Theory," *Strategic Management Journal* 4/4 (1983): 325–40; R. K. Kazanjian and R. Drazin, "A Stage Contingent Model of Design and Growth for Technology Based New Ventures," *Journal of Business Venturing* 5/3 (1990): 137–50; L. L. Steinmetz, "Critical Stages of Small Business Growth: When They Occur and How to Survive Them," *Business Horizons* 12/1 (1969): 29–36.

15. "Savvy Salutes America's 60 Top Women," *Savvy* 8 (Nov. 1987): 52–56.

16. Karen Barrett, "A New Breed of Entrepreneur" *Ms.* 12 (Jan. 1984): 23–24.

17. R. J. Fletcher, "Women Who Made Homework Pay," *Cosmopolitan* 197 (Dec. 1984): 222–26.

18. Names have been changed.

19. R. H. Brockhaus, "The Psychology of the Entrepreneur," in C. A. Kent, D. L. Sexton, and K. H. Vesper, eds. *Encyclopedia of Entrepreneurship* (Englewood

Cliffs, N.J.: Prentice-Hall, 1982), pp. 39–56; R. H. Brockhaus, "Effect of Job Dissatisfaction on the Decision to Start a Business," *Journal of Small Business Management* 18/1 (1980): 37–43; C. R. Stoner and F. E. Fry, "The Entrepreneurial Decision: Dissatisfaction or Opportunity?" *Journal of Small Business Management* 20/2 (1982): 39–44.

10

Conclusion

The central concern of this book has been the profitable strategies and management practices of small companies. This and related issues that we have examined are not unlike the questions raised and answered by the previous research on large businesses, notably by the Profit Impact of Marketing Strategy (PIMS) researchers, who have studied nearly three thousand relatively large businesses. Those researchers identified "strategy principles"—"principles that can help managers understand and predict how strategic choices and market conditions will affect business performance."[1]

Based on studies of over five hundred small companies, we have identified:

- Overall profiles of profitable businesses
- Strategies and practices that are profitable in different competitive environments
- Profitable strategies in growing, mature, and declining industries
- Profitable strategies in cyclical industries
- Profiles of firms that are start-ups, buy-outs, and inherited family firms
- Strategies that are profitable at different organizational life stages
- Strategies to perpetuate family firms
- Profiles of profitable women-owned small companies

THE PRINCIPLES OF PROFITABILITY

1. Overall, as shown in Figure 10.1, cash management and innovativeness are the most important competences that enhance the profitability of the firm.

While competence in cash management can be learned, innovativeness may be tied to the ability of the owner-manager and the people in the firm. The strength to innovate may be a lot harder to "buy" in the marketplace. A firm may not be able to sustain innovativeness over a period of time due to such factors as burn-out in creativity and turnover of key personnel.

2. Overall, as shown in Figure 10.2, the productivity of employees does not contribute much to the profitability of small companies. Indeed, only losing firms tend to emphasize efficiency

A firm's ability to realize high levels of efficiency depends on its ability to achieve economies of scale—economies associated with a large volume of sales. Small companies, in general, cannot achieve these economies and, therefore, efficiency per se cannot be a source of competitive advantage

3. Overall, as shown in Figure 10.3, broad product scope contributes to firm performance.

Product scope calls for complex organizational structure. Considering that small companies usually lack bargaining power to influence distributors, small company owners must be prepared to deal with the situation and move the company's products. Inability to secure supportive distributors will surely kill even a good product.

4. Overall, as shown in Figure 10.4, competitive position on product quality and administrative and selling costs have the most impact on firm performance.

Small companies with relatively high product quality tend to be the most profitable. High quality, as should be expected, goes together with relatively high prices and relatively high wages and salaries of key employees. High prices and high wages and salaries in themselves do not diminish the competitive position of the firm as long as the high prices and wages are commensurate with quality of the products. Relatively high administrative and selling costs, however, drag down firm profitability.

Figure 10.1
Cash Management, Innovativeness, and Profitability

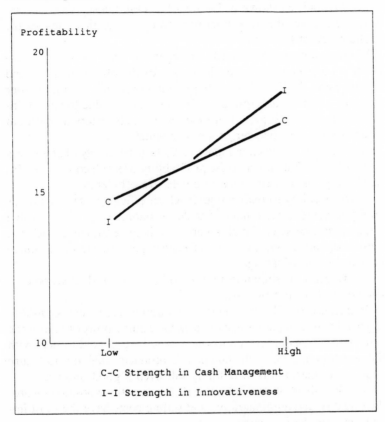

In sum, mean and lean small companies are profitable. They do not skimp on product quality, do not compete on price alone, and attract a quality-oriented workforce. Indeed, they build competitive advantage in product quality and position themselves as quality manufacturers.

5. Form and intensity of competition have an effect on firm performance. Profitable strategies tend to vary across competitive settings.

As shown in Figure 10.5, in low price and promotion competition, reliance on technology—notably patents and other rather restricted

Figure 10.2
Employee Productivity and Profitability

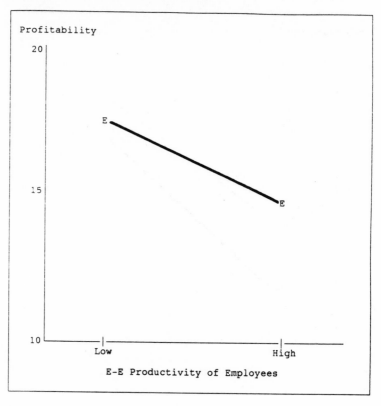

E-E Productivity of Employees

know-how—impedes firm performance. Profitable firms depend on generally accessible technologies rather than highly specialized know-how with limited applications.

In the relative absence of both price and promotion competition, profitable firms pursue the strategy of geographical focus, concentrating on local markets (markets located within one hundred miles of the firm). Business location, then, is the most important strength. To profitably serve regional and national markets that are far from the home base may require a large, complex organizational

Figure 10.3
Product Scope and Profitability

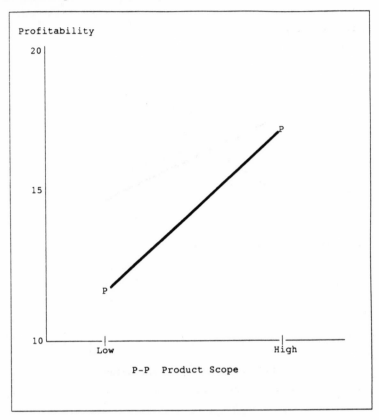

structure and certain economies of scale that usually go beyond the capabilities of most small firms.

Reliance on local markets ties the fortunes of the firm to local market conditions. Monitoring the local conditions and adapting to changes in the markets is the key to staying alive in competition-free settings. Markets do not stay free of competition forever.

6. In price-competitive settings, as shown in Figure 10.6, strategies of cost leadership and geographical focus contribute to profit.

Figure 10.4
Product Quality, Administrative/Sales Costs, and Profitability

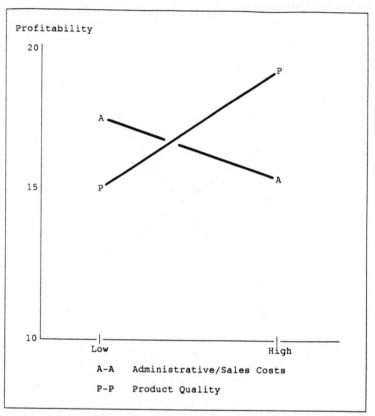

Price-competitive settings generally yield low profits. In order for a firm to be profitable in such inherently unattractive settings, it should be able to lower its costs and achieve high efficiency. Considering that small companies do not enjoy scale economies, the demands placed on them by the price-competitive environment cannot be easily met. Small firms in price-competitive settings could be the most vulnerable due to their inability to sustain their cost leadership strategy.

7. In a promotion-competitive environment, profitable firms, as shown in Figure 10.7, pursue the strategy of product quality and scope.

Figure 10.5
Technology, Geographical Focus, and Profitability in Low Price-/Promotion-Competitive Environments

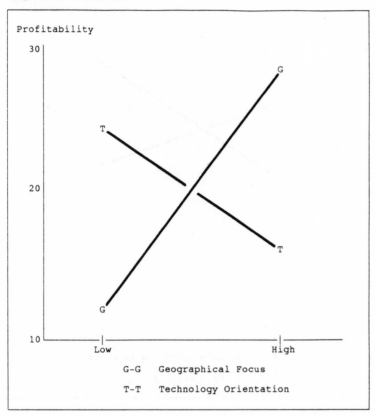

This strategy is appropriate as the environment really demands differentiation from each rival in the marketplace.

Small firms achieve this differentiation by emphasizing product quality, working to build a strong image, attracting and retaining quality employees by paying high wages and salaries, and deemphasizing new product introductions. The trick is to achieve differentiation by offering a variety of high-quality, familiar products, each catering

Figure 10.6
**Cost Leadership, Geographical Focus, and Profitability in
Price-Competitive Environments**

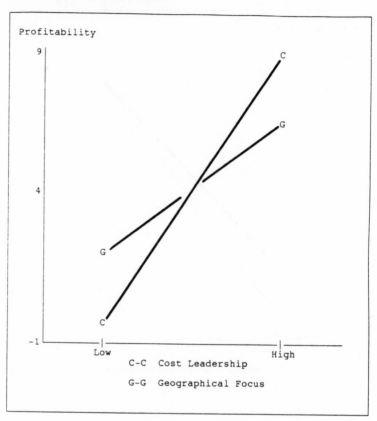

to a distinct market segment. Quiet quality leadership is the most profitable response in promotion-competitive environments.

8. In competitive settings where both price and promotion competition is intense, as shown in Figure 10.8, technology-oriented strategy is a drag on profit whereas geographical focus strategy tends to have a positive impact. The winning strategies are not unlike the combination of efforts that were identified under relatively competition-free environments.

Figure 10.7
Product Scope/Innovativeness and Profitability in Promotion-Competitive Environments

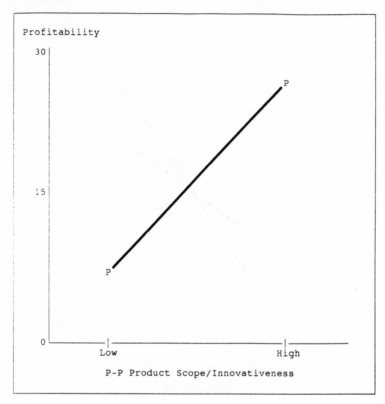

It is worth noting that there is a general lack of variety in the strategies that are associated with profit. For small firms the options are few: in promotion-competitive environments it is product scope and quality; in price-competitive environments, the options are cost leadership and geographical focus; in other settings the option is geographical focus.

While the narrow range of options tends to restrict the strategic discretion of owners-managers, the task of adapting strategy to

Figure 10.8
Technology Orientation, Geographical Focus, and Profitability in High Price-/Promotion-Competitive Environments

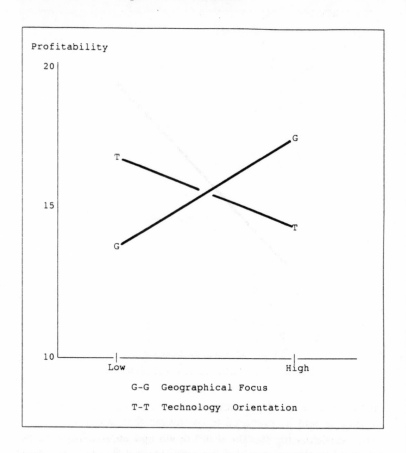

competitive environments may be much simpler for the smaller firm. A few well-honed strategies may serve small firms in a variety of settings.

9. A broad product line, as shown in Figure 10.9, is the key to profitability in high-growth environments. The idea is to take full advantage of the opportunities presented by the growth. Ability to

Figure 10.9
Breadth of Product Line and Profitability in Growing Industries

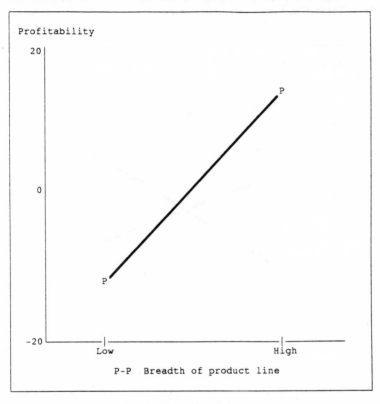

offer a wide range of products can be a constraint for small firms and they should be prepared to overcome that limitation.

10. As a growing market slows down and approaches maturity, quality of personnel can make a significant difference. In mature markets, as shown in Figure 10.10, profitable firms attract high-quality personnel by paying relatively high wages and salaries.

11. In declining industries, a broad product line is even more crucial. As shown in Figure 10.11, when industry is in a decline, offering a wide range of products helps a firm retain its customer base and remain profitable.

Figure 10.10
Wages/Salaries and Profitability in Mature Industries

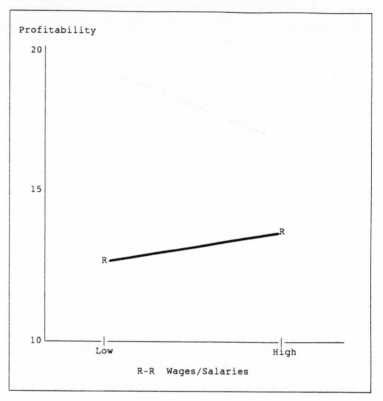

While adaptation to changing industry environments requires flexibility, a broad scope and single-minded commitment to high quality are the ingredients of the recipe for high profitability.

12. Financial flexibility—the ability to adjust finances of the firm to accommodate the changing demand conditions—is the key strength of profitable firms operating in cyclical industries. Owners-managers can make do with a little less provided they practice incremental planning and engage in intense boundary spanning, but the impact of financial flexibility cannot be matched by either method of planning or

Figure 10.11
Breadth of Product Line and Profitability in Declining Industries

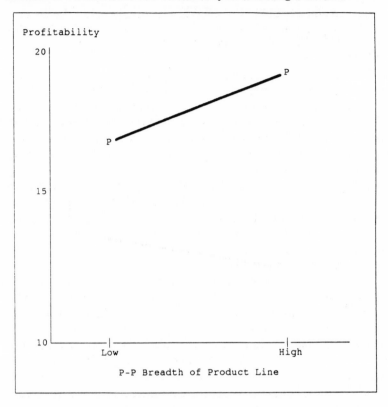

intensity of boundary spanning. Financial flexibility buffers a firm
from demand swings.

The importance of financial flexibility imposes the critical task of
liquidity management on the firm's owners-managers. This task
assumes different importance depending on the overall resources of
the firm, the stage of the business cycle, the extent to which the firm
is impacted by the business cycle, and ultimately, the owners'-
managers' risk profile. Obviously, a young, cash-poor firm in the
early stages of an economic downturn in a highly cyclical housing

industry, should be exercising greater caution than its very liquid counterpart. The aggressive entrepreneur needs to be especially careful of the desire to reinvest into ill-liquid assets all of the profits made during the good years. While such a tendency is the stuff of which business folk heroes are made, it is also the stuff that fills the records of the bankruptcy courts.

Financial flexibility needs to be increased as a period of economic expansion grows older, whereas financial flexibility can be spent (or invested) at the early stages of an economic upturn. Successful firms do not take actions that reduce their financial flexibility, with the hope that economic forecasts will warn them of an industry downturn. Economic forecasting is just too inexact to bet the future of the company on it.

13. Relative wages and salaries paid to key employees, as shown in Figure 10.12, can make a significant difference to the profitability of start-up firms. Ability to attract and retain high-caliber personnel is more critical to start-up firms than to either buy-out or inherited family firms. The competitive advantage of start-ups depends on the quality of the personnel.

14. In contrast to the above, breadth of product line and innovativeness, as shown in Figures 10.13 and 10.14, make a significant difference to inherited family firms. Most family firms, due to their old age, lose their ability to innovate and offer a broad range of products. Those firms that are able to retain flexibility to innovate and offer a broad scope of products will emerge as winners.

15. The performance of small companies, as shown in Figure 10.15, peaks as they approach middle age and drops as the firms enter the senior-citizen group. Accordingly, strategies and management practices tend to vary across the young, middle-aged, and senior groups of firms.

16. The senior citizens, as shown in Figure 10.16, tend to outperform juniors and middle-aged firms. Profitability of middle-aged and senior firms tends to be least affected by the industry conditions. Advanced age brings an element of robustness and staying power that juniors often lack.

17. Family businesses do not perpetuate themselves automatically. Deliberate strategic planning on the part of the owner-manager to

Figure 10.12
Wages/Salaries and Profitability in SUs, BOs, and FFs

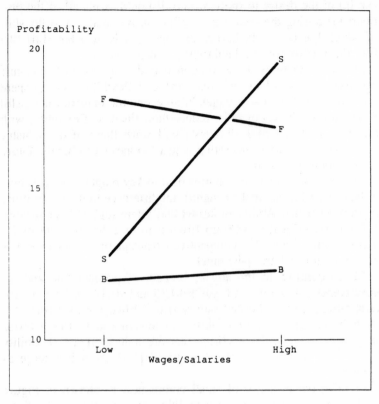

B-B   Buy-Outs

S-S   Start-Ups

F-F   Family Firms

continue the business, using a legal will to communicate the intention and aligning strategic and continuity planning are keys to successful perpetuation of a family firm.

While it may be tempting to think of business perpetuation efforts in terms of legal or tax efforts, many family businesses report a higher

Figure 10.13
Innovativeness and Profitability in SUs, BOs, and FFs

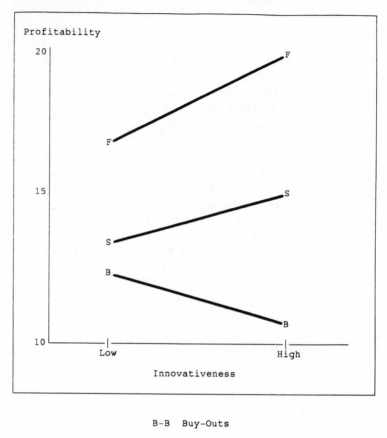

B-B   Buy-Outs
S-S   Start-Ups
F-F   Family Firms

degree of difficulty in interpersonal areas, such as designating a successor or communications among family members. Recognition of this problem is especially important for family business advisors, such as accountants and attorneys, who have regular and ongoing contact

Figure 10.14
Breadth of Product Line and Profitability in SUs, BOs, and FFs

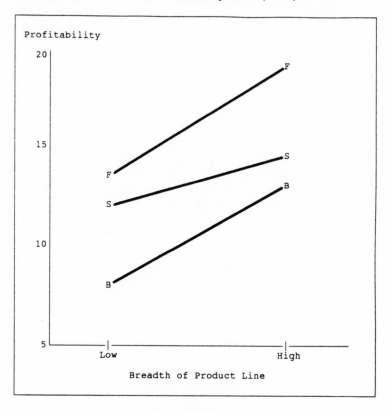

B-B   Buy-Outs
S-S   Start-Ups
F-F   Family Firms

with the business. It is critical that these specialists adopt a broader perspective than their family business clients. Of course, no single advisor is likely to have the entire spectrum of business expertise that might be required in a difficult situation, but at a minimum, the

Figure 10.15
Life Stages and Profitability

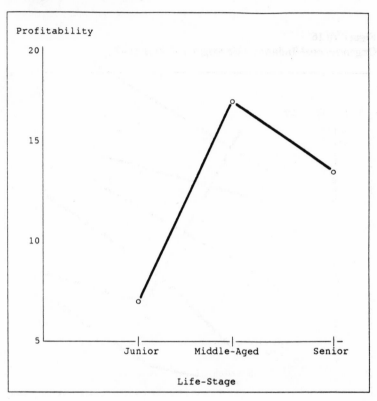

advisor should realize the limits of his or her contribution and be willing to suggest additional resources. Even the most sophisticated estate planning may be found wanting in the perpetuation effort if the interpersonal matters are ignored.

18. Profitable small women-owned firms, as shown in Figure 10.17, tend to be low-market share businesses, selling a large percent of sales through distributors, and generally competing on price.

Figure 10.16
Organizational/Industry Life Stages and Profitability

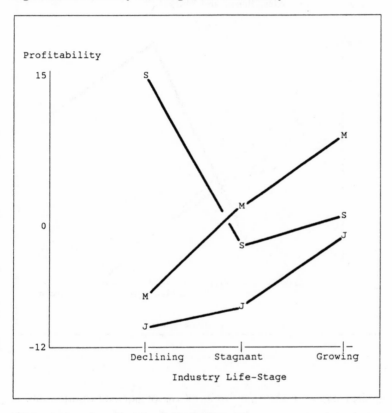

J-J   Junior

M-M   Middle-Aged

S-S   Senior

Figure 10.17
Profile of WOEs: Sales, Price, and Market Share

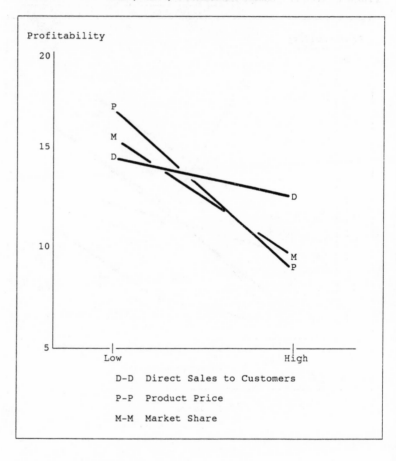

Figure 10.18
Profile of WOEs: Quality, Innovativeness, and Sales

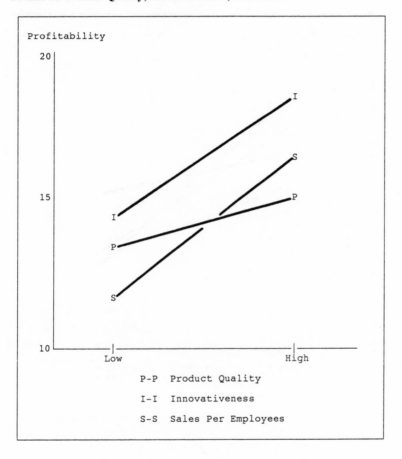

167

Figure 10.19
Consideration Style and Profitability in WOEs

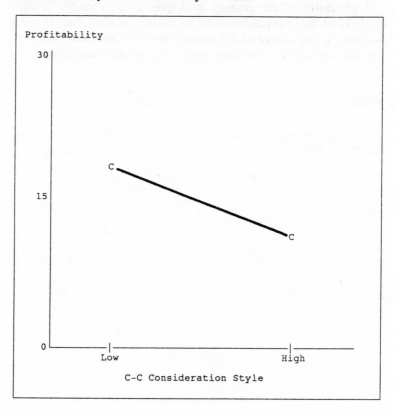

19. Profitable small firms, as shown in Figure 10.18, emphasize product quality, innovation, and sales per employee, and do not seek to minimize cost of production.

20. Women who own profitable small firms, as shown in Figure 10.19, exhibit a relative lack of consideration for people. These women expect their employees to be as results-oriented as themselves.

Applicability of the strategy principles to a particular business depends on the characteristics of the industry that the firm is doing business in, the nature of the product that the firm deals with, and the characteristics of the firm itself, among other variables.

NOTE

1. Robert D. Buzzell and Bradley T. Gates. *The PIMS Principles* (New York: Free Press, 1987).

Appendix 1

The Research Study

In the small business world, there are few objective sources of data. *Standard and Poor's* or *Moody's* directories of large, publicly held corporations and sources such as the *Robert Morris Associates' Annual Statement Studies,* which deal with small companies, do not provide data for individual firms. The Dun & Bradstreet's *Canadian Key Business Directory,* from which our study's list of firms was drawn, has extensive gaps in the employment and sales data. There is also a paucity of data bases like the PIMS.

Further, it is widely acknowledged that even if objective accounting data were available from small business establishments, the definitions and measurements of individual items vary across firms. These variations severely limit the comparability of the information.

While standardized objective data are clearly preferable, in the absence of such data, self-reported data can provide useful results. In fact, G. G. Dess and R. M. Robinson's findings show that the judgments of an owner-manager accurately reflect a firm's objective performance.[1] The use of such survey-based data is common in small business research, given the stage of development of this field.[2] Hence, self-reported data were used in this book.

The questions raised in Chapters 2, 3, 4, 6, 7, and 9 were examined with the help of data collected from 532 small manufacturing firms—340 in the United States and 192 in Canada. Owners-managers actively managed their business in these firms and employed one hundred or fewer individuals.

The data were collected using a structured mailed questionnaire. The questionnaire was pretested on twelve owners-managers of small manufacturing firms and was revised based on the responses. A copy of the questionnaire is in Appendix 2.

Very briefly, the following is a profile of the companies surveyed: On average, the firms were in business for 15 years, employed 19 persons, reported $658,000 in sales, and earned 16.23 percent a year.

NOTES

1. G. G. Dess, and R. M. Robinson, "Measuring Performance in Absence of Objective Measures," *Strategic Management Journal* 5 (1984): 265–74.

2. J. A. Hornaday, and N. C. Churchill, "Current Trends in Emtrepreneurial Research," in N. C. Churchhill et al., eds., *Frontiers of Entrepreneurship Research* (Wellesley, Mass.: Center for Entrepreneurship Studies, Babson College, 1987).

Appendix 2

Sample Questionnaire

A1. Managers pursue different kinds of goals for their businesses. Following is a list of eight such goals. Please take a minute to go through the items.

1. Profit
2. Growth of investments in the firm
3. Market share
4. Excellence of the quality of goods and services
5. Survival of business
6. Image of the firm in the immediate community
7. Owner's personal satisfaction with the business
8. Employee morale

Now some of these items would be more important to you than others. Identify *two* items which are "most important," another two items which are "somewhat important," and yet another two which are "not so important." Indicate your response by writing the numbers identifying the items in appropriate columns below.

Most Important	Somewhat Important	Somewhat Unimportant	Not So Important

A2. Personal satisfaction obtained from setting up and running one's firm is often a reason why owners-managers start their firms. All things considered, how would you rate the *personal satisfaction* you have derived from your career so far as an owner-manager? Check in one of the blanks below which best describes your response.

Very Satisfactory	Somewhat Satisfactory	Somewhat Unsatisfactory	Very Unsatisfactory
[ ]	[ ]	[ ]	[ ]

B1. Every firm has what one might call areas of *strength* and another set called areas of *weakness*. The following is a list of such areas. Please take a minute to go over the items.

1. Location of plant
2. Cash management
3. Product pricing
4. Product quality
5. Overall image of the firm
6. Customer service
7. Innovativeness of the firm
8. Marketing (including selling, promotion, and distribution)
9. Control of manufacturing costs
10. Inventory control
11. Quality control operations
12. Production capacity of plant and machinery
13. Customer credit policies
14. Productivity of employees
15. Types of markets served
16. Overall managerial competence of the executives

Now categorize the items into four groups—the items which you think represent areas of "major strength," "modest strength," "modest weakness," and "major weakness," and write down the identification numbers of the items in the appropriate columns below. Please make sure to identify *at least three* items in each column.

Areas of Major Strength	Areas of Modest Strength	Areas of Modest Weakness	Areas of Major Weakness

B2. How often your firm introduced *new products or made major changes* in old products during the last three years? Check in one of the blanks below.

About once every six months   ____

About once every year   ____

Periodically, but at intervals
longer than on year   ____

Not in the last three years   ____

C1. Every firm faces certain conditions which in a way help the firm do better on major goals or constrain the firm from doing better. Based on your experience during the last three years, rate each of the following items on degree to which each has helped or constrained *your firm* to do, say 10 percent, on the major goal of the firm. Circle a number between *1* and *4* to indicate your answer.

	The item was a:			
	Very limiting factor	*Limiting factor*	*Helpful factor*	*Very helpful factor*
Availability of raw material	1	2	3	4
Availability of investment capital	1	2	3	4
Availability of working capital	1	2	3	4
Availability of personnel	1	2	3	4
Production capacity of plant and machinery	1	2	3	4
Availability of fuels and energy	1	2	3	4
Sales outlook in the industry	1	2	3	4

C2. How would you describe the breadth of the product or service line of your firm relative to the product or service line of your *leading competitors*? Breadth of the line refers to the number of *different* types of products or services offered by a firm. Check in one of the blanks below.

Much, much broader	Broader	Narrower	Much, much Narrower
[ ]	[ ]	[ ]	[ ]

D1. In the particular industry in which your firm is operating, how intense is the competition in each of the following? Circle a number between *1* and *4* which describes the actual condition in the industry. In answering consider the competition you face from both *large* and *small* firms.

	Negligible	Somewhat Negligible	Intense	Extremely Intense
Inputs or purchases of items like raw materials, parts, and equipment	1	2	3	4
Technical manpower such as engineers, accountants, machine operators	1	2	3	4
Promotion, distribution, advertising, selling	1	2	3	4
Price	1	2	3	4

D2. As an owner-manager you must have dealt directly or indirectly with one or more public agencies at federal, provincial, and municipal levels. Based on your experience, how helpful was each of the following public agencies to your firm? Circle a number between *1* and *4* which best describes your experience.

	Very Helpful	Helpful	Unhelpful	Very Unhelpful
Agencies of the federal government	4	3	2	1
Agencies of the state government	4	3	2	1
Agencies of the municipal government	4	3	2	1

E1. Relative to leading competitors—big or small—how would you rate your performance in each of the following. Consider the picture during the last three years while making these comparison. Indicate your response by circling a number between *1* and *4*.

	Much Lower	Somewhat Lower	Somewhat Higher	Much Higher
Administration and selling costs	1	2	3	4
Product prices	1	2	3	4
Wage and salary level of employees	1	2	3	4
Profit or loss as a percent of total assets of the firm	1	2	3	4
Manufacturing costs	1	2	3	4

	Much Lower	Somewhat Lower	Somewhat Higher	Much Higher
Product quality	1	2	3	4
Image of the firm	1	2	3	4
Quality of customer service	1	2	3	4
Overall managerial competence	1	2	3	4

E2. During the past year has the firm made (check one below):

Profits   ____

Losses   ____

F1. Roughly what was the profit (or loss) during the *past year*? Express the profit (or loss) as a percentage of the total assets of the firm. Consider the past year's figure only. Place a check in one of the blanks which best describes your answer.

Less than 5% ____   6–10% ____ 11–15% ____ 16–20% ____ 21–30% ____
31–40% ____   41–50% ____ 51–60% ____ 61–70% ____ 71–80% ____
81–90% ____ 91–100% ____   More than 100% ____

F2. Approximately what percent of your firm's sales are made to each of the following? Write the percentages in the blanks.

Directly to customers   ____

To wholesalers   ____

To retailers   ____

F3. Are the major products and services offered by your firm (check in one of the blanks below):

More or less standardized for all customers   ____

Designed and produced to specification   ____

F4. Does your firm use patents, trade secrets, or other proprietary methods of production or operation? Check in the appropriate blank.

Pertaining to product   Yes ____   No ____

Pertaining to process   Yes ____   No ____

F5. How many years of formal education did you complete? Circle a number which best represents your answer.

7 or less 8   9   10   11   12   13   14   15   16   17   18   19   20+

F6. Indicate the approximate number of employees in your firm by checking in one of the blanks.

10 or less ____   11–24 ____   25–49 ____   50–75 ____   76–99   ____
100–199 ____ 200–299 ____ 300–399 ____ 400–499 ____ 500 or more ____

G1. Indicate the approximate average *annual sales* (in thousands of dollars) of your firm in the last three years by checking in one of the blanks.

50 or less _____   51–99 _____   100–199 _____   200–299 _____   300–399 _____
400–499 _____   500–599 _____   600–699 _____   700–799 _____   800–899 _____
900–999 _____   1–1.5 million _____   Over 1.5 million _____

G2. During the last year, roughly what percentage of your firm's sales were made to customers or buyers in the following areas?

To customers or buyers within about
one hundred miles of your plant   _____

To customers in the rest of region   _____

To customers in the rest of country   _____

To customers outside the country   _____

G3. Owners-managers like you keep track of what is going on in the firm by looking at various aspects of the business. Some of the items that they keep track of are listed below.

Please take a minute to go over the items.

1. Accounts receivable and payable
2. Manufacturing costs of all major products
3. Profits rates of all major products
4. Quality control of major products
5. Inventory levels of all major items
6. Cash flow
7. Labor productivity
8. Labor costs
9. Plant capacity
10. Sales of all major products

H1. Managers keep track of these items in different ways—some prepare and review reports regularly while others may keep track of the things more informally. Now categorize the items listed above into three groups shown below based on the *practice* followed for each item in *your* organization. Write down the number corresponding to each item in the most appropriate column to mark your answers.

	In the following items:	
"We prepare reports and review them regularly"	"The following is all in books. And we can call for the reports as and when needed"	"We know what is going on and do not need to keep records"

H2. Sometimes owners-managers plan well ahead of time in each of their business activities. *How far ahead* do you plan for each of the following? Circle a number between *1* and *4* which is the most appropriate number for each item.

	Less than 3 months	3–6 months	6–12 months	More than 1 year
Sales	1	2	3	4
Manufacturing costs	1	2	3	4
Volume of production	1	2	3	4
Inventories	1	2	3	4
Cash flows	1	2	3	4
Advertising and other selling expenditures	1	2	3	4
Introduction of new products	1	2	3	4
Entry into new markets	1	2	3	4
Manpower	1	2	3	4
Capital for expansions, purchase of plant and equipment	1	2	3	4

J1. Small businesses sometimes use outside help to solve some specific problems faced by them. For each of the following items, indicate whether your firm has used professional management help from outside within the last *two* years by circling the number which is the most appropriate. Consider any help received from individual consultants, consulting firms, or governmental agencies as relevant for this purpose.

	Yes	No
In obtaining grants and loans on special terms	1	0
In setting up accounting and bookkeeping methods	1	0
In recruiting personnel	1	0

	Yes	No
In estimating demand and identifying markets	1	0
In controlling costs of manufacturing and marketing	1	0
In controlling inventories	1	0
In managing labor relations	1	0
In handling matters of taxation	1	0
In designing and modifying products	1	0
In planning new products and dropping the old ones	1	0
In solving urgent and unexpected problems	1	0
In day-to-day paper work	1	0
In dealing with government agencies	1	0
In planning expansions and long-term investments	1	0

K1. How many of your product manufacturing establishments are in cities, towns, and villages? Write the numbers in the appropriate blanks.

In cities _____ In towns _____ In villages _____

K2. In which year did you buy or start the firm?

_____ (year)

K3. Briefly describe the nature of the product and services of the firm in the space given below.

_____

K4. Do you employ one or more individuals who are qualified or experienced to assist you in each of the following activities? For each item, place a check in the most appropriate blank.

Supervise production	Yes _____	No _____
Selling	Yes _____	No _____
Bookkeeping	Yes _____	No _____
Office management	Yes _____	No _____
Plant maintenance	Yes _____	No _____

K5. Approximately how many customers are served by your firm? Check in the most appropriate blank.

3 or fewer _____   4–9 _____   10–19 _____

20–49 _____   50–99 _____   100–999 _____

1000–9999 _____   10,000 or more _____

L1. Have you attended management training programs in the following areas? Place a check in the appropriate blank for each item.

	Yes	No
Starting of new ventures	_____	_____
Accounting, bookkeeping	_____	_____
Marketing, selling	_____	_____
Investment, credit, or cash management	_____	_____
General management for small businesses	_____	_____
Other. (Please specify.)	_____	_____

L2. Roughly, what is the ratio of current assets to current liabilities of the firm? Consider the past year's figure only.

Note: *Current assets* are the sum total of inventories, cash, and accounts receivable. *Current liabilities* are the sum total of short-term debts, accounts payable, and taxes payable.

Circle a number below which best describes your answer.

¼ ½ ¾ 1 1¼ 1½ 1¾ 2

3 4 5 6 7 8 9 10 More than 10

L3. Based on what has been happening to sales in your industry during the past three years, which one of the following best describes the situation? Check in one of the blanks below.

Industry sales are just starting to grow _____

Industry sales are growing at 10 percent a year or more _____

Industry sales are neither growing nor declining _____

Industry sales are beginning to decline _____

Industry sales are declining at 10 percent a year or more _____

L4. Looking at the next three years, do you think the situation will continue, improve, or get worse? Check in one of the blanks below.

Will continue   ____
Will improve   ____
Will get worse   ____

M1. Which of the following best describes the manner in which you have come into the management of the firm? Check in one of the blanks.

Started the firm from scratch   ____
Bought it from an outsider   ____
The firm has been in the family for some time now   ____

M2. How many years of experience do you have in the current line of business? Consider the years you were an entrepreneur, as well as the years you might have worked in another firm in the same line of business. Circle a number which best represents your answer.

1   2   3   4   5   6   7   8   9   10   11–15   16–20   21+

MANY THANKS FOR YOUR COOPERATION!

If you would like a copy of the findings write your mailing address below. A summary of the findings will be available in four months.

_____

_____

_____

Index

Index

About the Authors

RAJESWARARAO CHAGANTI is currently the chairperson of the Department of General and Strategic Management, School of Business and Management, Temple University. He is an electrical engineer by training, received his graduate degree in management from the Indian Institute of Management, Calcutta, and a Ph.D. in management from the State University of New York, Buffalo. He is an alumnus of the Graduate School of Business Administration, Harvard University, where he attended the International Teachers Program.

Dr. Chaganti teaches business policy and strategic management, among other management courses, and has extensive experience in teaching executive development programs.

Dr. Chaganti's research interests are in business strategies for small companies, and the influence of top executives and the corporate board of directors on business policy and business strategies. He has written extensively on small company management, entrepreneurship, top management characteristics, corporate boards of directors, and social issues in management. His research writings have been accepted for publication in the *Strategic Management Journal,* the *Journal of Management Studies*, the *Journal of Small Business Management*, and *Entrepreneurship: Theory and Practice* (formerly the *American Journal of Small Business*), among other research publications.

RADHA CHAGANTI is an associate professor of business policy and environmental analysis, School of Business Administration, Rider College. She did her graduate work in management at the Indian Institute of Management, Calcutta, and received her Ph.D. from the State University of New York, Buffalo. She has extensive experience in the administration of a small business development center.

Dr. Radha Chaganti's teaching interests are in business policy, strategic management, and small business management. Her research interests are in business policy, strategic management, small business management and entrepreneurship, and women-owned and -operated small companies. Her research has been accepted for publication in the *Journal of Small Business Management* and *Entrepreneurship: Theory and Practice* (formerly the *American Journal of Small Business*) and *Advance in Strategic Management*, among other journals.

STEWART C. MALONE is currently an assistant professor at the McIntire School of Commerce at the University of Virginia. Dr. Malone received his B.B.A. from Roanoke College, an M.B.A. from Pennsylvania State University, and a Ph.D. from Temple University.

Prior to joining the University of Virginia, Dr. Malone served sixteen years as president of his family business with over $2 million in sales. Founded in 1854, his firm is one of the older small companies still owned and operated by the family of the original founder.

Dr. Malone now teaches strategic management, small business management, entrepreneurship and new ventures, and does research in those areas. His research was accepted for publication in the *Journal of Small Business Management, Family Business Review,* and the *Journal of Business Venturing.* He contributes frequently to practitioner-oriented publications and conducts executive development programs.